QUEST

FOR THE ORIGINS OF THE

FIRST

AMERICANS

QUEST

FOR THE ORIGINS OF THE

FIRST

AMERICANS

E. JAMES DIXON

UNIVERSITY OF NEW MEXICO PRESS

ALBUQUERQUE

Library of Congress cataloging–in–Publiction Data

Dixon, E. James.
    Quest for the origins of the first Americans / E. James Dixon
        p. cm.
    Includes bibliographical references (p.   ) and index.
    ISBN 0–8263–1480-5
    1. Indians—Origin. 2. Indians—Asian influences. 3. Paleo—
Indians—North America. 4. Bering Land Bridge—History. 5.
Alaska—Antiquities. 6. North America—Antiquities. I. Title.
E61.D59   1992
970.01—dc20   92–26146
                                                        CIP

This book is dedicated to my friend and colleague, Dick Jordan, who died shortly before it was finished. With his passing the North lost a dedicated archeologist and teacher.

CONTENTS

ILLUSTRATIONS

Illustrations

PREFACE

 This book has three major themes. The first and most important is the documentation, synthesis, and interpretation of the early prehistory of the western North American arctic and subarctic. The archeology of this region is important in world prehistory because it is here that both North America and Asia were repeatedly connected by a land bridge. It is also the area where the eastern and western hemispheres come closest to one another. This geographic proximity and past physical connections mean that plants, animals, peoples, and ideas have been able to move between the two hemispheres with relative ease.

The second theme of this book is the process of scientific inquiry. I have endeavored to share the excitement of discovery and the social context of intellectual growth. Information exchanged between colleagues and the discovery of new data and techniques shape the character of scientific interpretation.

There are fundamentally two types of scientific inquiry: that which follows established and approved procedures of a discipline, and that which extends the boundaries of science through innovation of new methods or discoveries. Some scientists do both; these are not mutually exclusive activities. Both types of research are essential. Scientists who move forward using standard methods and techniques expand the breadth of our knowledge by documenting the age, nature, and geographic distribution of sites. Scientists who bring forth unexpected discoveries and introduce new methods or concepts frequently challenge the premises of the discipline and may be perceived as threatening the security of the established and familiar intellectual order of archeology. Consequently, this book also is about risk taking and the courage required to face rejection and criticism.

The third theme is the history of archeology in Alaska. I feel fortunate to be part of the continuum of northern archeologists.

xi

Preface

Many of the earlier generation of scientists working on the archeology of the North touched my life as teachers and mentors, including Doug Anderson, Dave Hopkins, Tom Hamilton, Helge Larsen, Robert McKennan, and John Cook. I have shared the experiences of graduate and postgraduate training, fieldwork, and mutual support with Chuck Holmes, Dick Jordan, Dennis Stanford, and many other scientists whose names are scattered throughout this book. I would like to pass on to younger archeologists and those who simply enjoy learning about this subject an appreciation for the scientists whose work forms the basis of our knowledge.

A synthesis such as this is possible only for the regional specialist, because many of the sources of information are not generally available. These include a vast array of unpublished reports, papers delivered at local and regional meetings, and unpublished manuscripts resulting from field research. The progressive accumulation of these types of data has accelerated during the past twenty years, as a result of archeological projects funded or required by government agencies. Unless one has been able to follow continuously these developments in conjunction with the progress of academic archeology, the prehistory of the western North American arctic and subarctic is incomprehensible. Although I have attempted to cite these sources whenever possible, I am sure that there are some that I have missed and others that I have chosen to ignore for the sake of relevance. Not only have I strived to pull together this vast array of scattered material, but I have imposed on it a framework that attempts to organize and to some degree explain these data. This is necessary not only to provide order to what otherwise would be a series of unrelated archeological site and artifact descriptions, but also to determine which of those reports and descriptions are relevant to the prehistory during this time period.

This book is directed to a broad and diverse audience including the lay reader, interested students, and professional archeologists. I frequently explain terms and concepts that would be unnecessary if this study were directed to a purely scientific audience. Though some of my colleagues may find this approach cumbersome, it will help the less specialized readers share in the archeological experiences and processes that many of us take for granted.

ACKNOWLEDGMENTS

Wherever possible, I have tried to credit the sources of ideas in this book. I would like to thank the University of Alaska Fairbanks for granting the sabbatical that enabled me to complete the manuscript. I would also like to acknowledge the help and encouragement I received in writing this book. Claire Sanderson, former editor of the University of New Mexico Press, first suggested this project, and Dennis Stanford reviewed the original outline. Claire's successor, Andrea Otañez, followed the publication process to completion. Sharon Olive typed the manuscript through its many drafts.

I thank David M. Hopkins for providing figure 1.3 and, along with Quaternary Research, for permission to reproduce figure 1.2. The Academy of Science, Magadan, of the former Soviet Union provided figure 3.4. Charles Schweger and Academic Press granted permission to use figure 3.5. Figure 7.1 was provided courtesy of Charles Mason. Figures 5.5 and 7.2 were provided by Roger Powers and Ted Goebel. Thomas Dillehay and *Scientific American* granted permission to reproduce figure 8.1. Along with authors Dillehay and Gideon, *Nature* granted permission to use figures 8.2 and 8.3. Permission to use these illustrations has improved the quality of the manuscript and the cooperation of these individuals and publishers is greatly appreciated.

I am grateful to Marilyn Jesmain, Bob Sattler, and Dixon Sims for their assistance in preparing many of the maps and line drawings. Barry McWayne provided valuable photographic expertise. Gary Selinger provided a variety of support important to completing this manuscript. Dave Morgan provided a variety of technical assistance for which I am grateful.

My work in Australia benefited from the generosity and assistance of George and Chriss Kenrick, Tom Loy, Rhys Jones and Alan Thorne. I wish to thank Tom Dillehay for reviewing chapter 8 and Tom Loy for reviewing chapters 6 and 9. The entire draft manuscript was reviewed and edited by my wife, Mim Dixon, to whom I owe

Acknowledgments

special thanks for her help and encouragement. Although all these people deserve credit for improving this book, I accept responsibility for any errors or interpretations that may ultimately prove to be bizarre.

CHAPTER 1

THE QUEST

On a cold October night we waded into the clear river in interior Alaska. The bright moon and our hissing gas lanterns illuminated the fast-flowing water. Wading deeper into the stream, we watched for the silver flash of spawning whitefish. My ten-year-old son, Bryan, looked toward the sky and called our attention to a magnificent display of the aurora borealis. The colors of the northern lights rippled through the sky like the shimmering water rippling around our legs. Bryan thrust his spear into the water. In one quick move he deftly pinned a whitefish to the gravel bottom of the stream.

I moved through the water to help him with the writhing fish. In the lantern light I saw a rivulet of blood from the speared fish mix with the clear river water. As the water splashed on the shafts of our spears it quickly froze, making our grip difficult and reducing our accuracy. Throughout the night we repeatedly thrust our spears into the water, catching many fish and missing many more. We were fishing in much the same manner as prehistoric people had fished for thousands of years, and it provided a basis for understanding the hardships and exhilaration that prehistoric people had experienced repeatedly throughout their lives.

At one o'clock in the morning we hiked back to the road and loaded our gear into the car. I gently tucked a very tired ten-year-old boy under a blanket. As I drove home with my son quietly sleeping in the back seat, my mind turned to the exciting adventure that would begin for me at midnight that same day. In this autumn of 1986 I was about to undertake another journey in an odyssey that had begun for me almost twenty years earlier, when I entered the search to resolve some questions concerning the origins of the first Americans.

This journey would lead me from Fairbanks, Alaska, to the nation's capital, the American Museum of Natural History in New York City, a geriatric hospital in British Columbia, and the conti-

1

Chapter 1

nent of Australia. Like the legendary search for the Holy Grail, the quest to understand the origins of the first Americans has an almost spiritual quality for the researchers involved. As with many great undertakings, the knowledge and experience derived in the pursuit of the goal is frequently more important than the goal itself.

As I drove home under the quiet canopy of the northern lights I thought about the efforts of the many scientists who sought to unlock the secrets of the universe. Understanding and experience derived from the process of scientific inquiry provide knowledge, which enriches our lives. Resolutions of scientific problems are goals scientists attempt to achieve through field and laboratory research, implementing rigorous scientific methods. However, as seasoned researchers soon learn, every problem solved leads to additional questions, theories, complexities, experiments, and discoveries. These, in turn, lead to the definition of additional problems and new discoveries. As long as human inventiveness and curiosity exist, there will be no ultimate explanation for the infinite array of phenomena and processes that surround us. But certainly these scientific endeavors increase our knowledge and enhance the physical and spiritual quality of our world.

* * * * * * *

Alaska is one of the best locations in North America to search for evidence of the first humans to inhabit the North American continent. Anthropologists favor the concept that early human populations first reached the New World from Asia via Alaska. Since the sixteenth century there has been a long tradition of scholarship leading to contemporary concepts explaining how human groups colonized the American continents. In 1589 Jesuit priest Joseph de Acosta published an important work synthesizing and interpreting his extensive travels during the 16 years he lived in the Americas. His residence in the New World was closely linked with the early phase of the expansion of the Spanish Empire in the New World.

Based on logical evaluation of biological and cultural information he had amassed, and remaining within the intellectual and religious parameters of his time, de Acosta defined three hypotheses that could explain how humans arrived in the Americas. His assumption that the human species originated in the Old World was derived from the Bible; he fully accepted that all humans had descended from Adam and that Adam had been created in the Old World. The three hypotheses he considered were deliberate and planned transoceanic voyages, accidental voyages, and migration via land. After carefully and logically evaluating each of these possibilities, de Acosta concluded that the Old World and New World either were connected by land or were in close proximity in the then-unexplored high northern latitudes.

Most importantly, de Acosta viewed the movement of humans into the Americas in conjunction with the movement of animals. After carefully considering the animal species in both the Americas and the Old World, de Acosta correctly reasoned that the animals could only have passed by a land connection between the two continents. He (de Acosta 1604:63) carried this reasoning to human populations by stating,

> We may easily inferre by these argumants [speaking of the similarities of the faunal communities] that the first Indians went to inhabit the Indies more by land then by sea; or if there were any navigation, it was neither great nor difficult, being an indubitable thing, that the one world is continued and joined with the other, or at the least they approach on neerer unto another in some parts.

De Acosta (1604:61) theorized that this movement into the Western Hemisphere was not deliberate but accomplished "without consideration in changing by little and little their lands and habitations. Some peopling the lands they found, and other seeking for newe, in time they came to inhabite the Indies." Contemporary anthropologists hold similar views and regard humans much as they would any other species that will expand its population, generation after generation into an unoccupied environment. Thus, the migration of humans to the New World is viewed as a gradual expansion of human population with ever-increasing numbers progressively colonizing unoccupied territory.

From the first insights of de Acosta, the necessity of a land connection between the two continents has been recognized as an

Chapter 1

essential prerequisite to explain the similarities in the biological communities between the two hemispheres. It logically follows that if a land connection was necessary to explain the distribution of plants and animals, then a land connection would also provide an avenue for human populations to spread from one hemisphere to the other. In an excellent review in 1933 of the development of anthropological theory pertinent to the earliest human colonization of the Americas, Spinden (1933:219–224) emphasized that the distribution of animals necessitated a land bridge, and the concept of a land bridge served as the guiding dictum in explaining the movement of humans from the Old World to the Americas. Thus, since Western scholars began to consider the problem, the study of the earliest humans to enter the Americas has been linked closely with studies in biology, paleontology, and geology.

Though archeologists and biologists generally agree on the movement of humans, plants, and animals between Asia and North America, they depend upon geologists to explain how and when a land bridge between the two continents existed in the past. In 1728 Vitus Bering established that Asia and North America were not connected by land, but it gradually became evident that a land connection between the two continents must have existed sometime in the remote past. By 1894 enough field data had been collected for G. M. Dawson to demonstrate that much of the Bering and Chukchi seas, including Bering Strait, was less than 600 feet deep. He realized that the underlying ocean floor stretching between Alaska and Siberia was physiographically part of the continental plateau and not part of the deep ocean basins. He reasoned that "in later geologic times more than once and perhaps during long periods a wide terrestrial plain connecting North America and Asia" had existed (Dawson 1894:143–144).

Louis Agassiz, a Swiss zoologist turned geologist, theorized from overwhelming evidence that glaciers, which are today largely restricted to mountainous areas, were once widespread throughout Europe. He visited America in 1846 and recognized that the geologic evidence demonstrated that massive ice sheets once covered much of North America. This interval in the history of the

The Quest

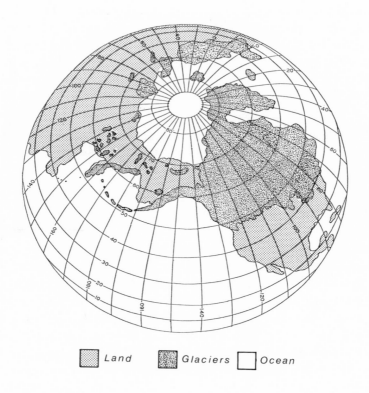

1.1 North America and northeast Asia during the height of the Wisconsin glaciation.

earth is the Pleistocene, popularly known as the Ice Ages. During the Pleistocene much of human evolution occurred and many large mammals existed, including mammoth, mastodon, and extinct types of bison and horse. The Pleistocene was punctuated by times when glaciers expanded, called glacials, and times when they retreated, called interglacials.

By 1933, W. A. Johnston, a geologist working for the Geological Survey of Canada, had synthesized much of the existing geological and paleontological information relevant to explaining how a land

Chapter 1

bridge formed between the two continents. Johnston (1933:31–32) observed:

> During the Wisconsin stage of glaciation the general level of the sea must have been lower owing to the accumulation of ice on the land. The amount of lowering is generally estimated to have been at least 180 feet, so that a land bridge probably existed during the height of the last glaciation . . . . During the waning of the last glaciation the sea gradually rose on the land, and together with erosion, may have opened the strait . . . . The Bering Strait region is well outside of any large glaciated area.

Logical reasoning and research by geologists provided other sciences with the explanation of how a land bridge had formed. The formation of the Bering Land Bridge is easily illustrated by drawing an analogy to a seesaw. On one side of the seesaw is glaciers and on the other is sea level. When glaciers expand or "go up," sea level goes down. When glaciers retreat or "go down," sea level goes up. That is, as immense amounts of the earth's water are transferred from the oceans to snow, which gradually accumulates as glacial ice, sea level is lowered. When the glaciers melt, the resultant water is transported back to the oceans by the earth's rivers, and sea level rises. The Bering Land Bridge formed as a result of lower sea level exposing the relatively shallow sea bed. There are other geologic means by which a land bridge might form, including movements of the earth's crust or crustal rebound after melting of the massive glaciers. Although these processes significantly affected regions near Bering Strait during the past, they were not processes that created the Land Bridge. Direct proof of the former land bridge has been established in recent years by the recovery of remains of extinct mammals dredged from the ocean floor (Dixon 1983), recognition of former river courses on the seafloor (McManus et al. 1983), and the occurrence of subaeral geologic deposits in cores taken from the ocean sediments (Hopkins 1967, McManus et al. 1983, Elias et al. 1991).

The continental shelf stretching beneath the Bering and Chukchi seas between Asia and North America is more than 1,000 kilometers wide. Approximately 18,000 years ago during the height of the last

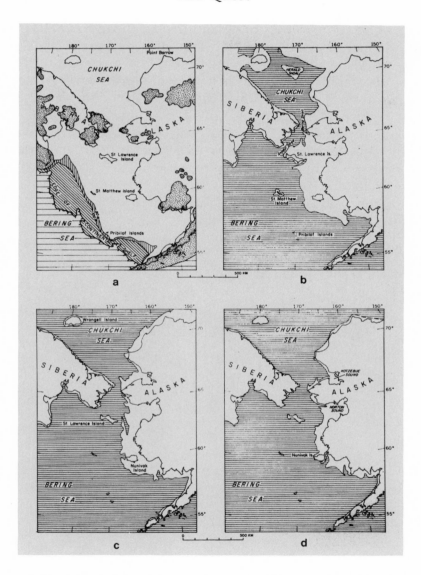

1.2 Sequence of sea level rise in the Bering Sea area. (a) The Bering Land Bridge at the height of the last glaciation; (b) partition of the land bridge, ca. 10,000 B.P.; (c,d) stages of Holocene sea level rise in Bering Strait, at minus 38 m and minus 30 m respectively (Hopkins 1973:524 reproduced with permission of Quaternary Research *and the author).*

Chapter 1

major glaciation, called the Wisconsin after the region in which it was first clearly identified, most of the continental shelf was exposed as dry land. The Bering Land Bridge was a vast region of low topographic relief with a few mountains, which are today islands in the Bering Sea, widely spaced across the landscape. The land bridge and adjacent areas of North America and Asia form a geographic area called Beringia. This region has been divided further into two provinces. The area lying in North America is referred to as eastern Beringia. Western Beringia is situated in Asia. When scientists speak of eastern Beringia, they are referring to the region that is today Alaska and adjacent areas of Canada that were not covered by the massive continental glaciers.

Between the early 1930s and the early 1960s, fieldwork by paleontologists, geologists, and botanists laid the foundation to understand the role of the Bering Land Bridge in the distribution of plants and animals. Concurrently archeologists recognized pronounced similarities between the archeological remains found in Alaska and Siberia. These progressive contributions to knowledge culminated in the publication of *The Bering Land Bridge* which was coordinated and edited by David M. Hopkins, a seasoned geologist with a remarkable talent for synthesizing diverse research findings. This important work presented research on the nature, character, and history of the land bridge. Based on the scanty data available at the time, Hopkins (1967:464–465) speculated that the former connection between Asia and North America was inundated by rising sea level for the last time sometime shortly after 10,000 years ago. This volume became the definitive work on the Bering Land Bridge for the next decade, during which time Hopkins encouraged many young geologists and archeologists, including me, to further explore this region.

It was evident to archeologists that a land connection between the two continents had existed in the not-too-distant past, probably when well-documented stone projectile points associated with the remains of extinct mammoths were being used in the more southern areas of North America. These distinctive stone artifacts are unique not only because they were used to hunt mammoth but because they were manufactured by removing a flake of stone from the base of the projectile point. By removing the stone in this manner, a flute was left on the projectile point, creating a unique or diagnostic characteristic. The earliest of these distinctive fluted projectile points are called Clovis points, after an important site at which they were found near Clovis, New Mexico.

These fluted projectile points were probably used to tip darts thrown with an atlatl, or spear thrower. The atlatl is an ingenious tool that serves as an artificial extension of the human arm and permits greater leverage to be applied when throwing a lightweight spear, or dart. This is important because it not only provides greater force but also increases the range of the weapon and provides greater safety when hunting potentially dangerous large mammals.

In 1948 geologist R. M. Thompson reported finding a fluted projectile point in northern Alaska that was strikingly similar to the Clovis points in the Southwest. Since then numerous other fluted points have been found in Alaska and adjacent Yukon Territory, Canada. Unfortunately all of the specimens from eastern Beringia have been found at sites where dates appear to be ambiguous or inaccurate or on the surface of the ground where it is impossible to date them using standard geological methods. Because of their similarity with the Clovis points to the south, some researchers have suggested that these projectile points are the tangible remains of the first people who crossed the Bering Land Bridge and subsequently spread south, hunting mammoths and other large mammals.

This model explaining human movement into the Americas in turn supports a theory that has been advanced to explain one of America's greatest mysteries: What caused so many large mammals to die at the end of the Pleistocene? In the Americas, approximately 70 genera became extinct in the past 15,000 years, including the large elephant-like mammoth and mastodon and several different types of bison and horse (Martin 1984). Paul S. Martin (1967, 1973, and 1984) has suggested that human hunters were responsible for the extinction of these large mammals. He postulates that as humans moved into the Americas they encountered large mammals that had never experienced human hunters and as a result had developed no effective means of evading these highly intelligent and sophisticated predators. He concludes that the large mammals were hunted to extinction in a relatively short period of time. By simulating human population growth rates for hunter and gatherers and estimating the amount of territory required to support human groups practicing this type of economy, Mossimann and Martin (1973) have demonstrated that humans could have colonized both North and South America in approximately 1,000 years and concurrently killed off the large Pleistocene mammals. This theory explaining Pleistocene extinctions is called the overkill hypothesis. Some scientists have argued that it was the dramatic change in climate that caused the extinctions, while others have suggested that a combination of both climatic change and human predation were the cause.

By the mid 1960s the weight of evidence indicated that a land bridge between Asia and North America had existed in the not-too-distant past. Archeological evidence from interior regions of North

1.3 View from Seward Peninsula, Alaska, across Bering Strait to the Diomede Islands and Cape Dezhnev, (far background) northeast Siberia (courtesy of David M. Hopkins).

The Quest

America clearly demonstrated that Clovis mammoth hunters were in North America at the close of the Pleistocene. Additionally, a number of artifacts and archeological sites, although not conclusive, strongly suggested the presence of humans in the Americas long before the firmly documented and widely accepted Clovis sites. There was little doubt that the first humans to enter the Americas came via the Bering Land Bridge, expanding into new territory and hunting the large Pleistocene mammals as they had done in the Old World where there were numerous, well-documented archeological sites. Like almost everyone else, I fully accepted this hypothesis and even wrote a Ph.D dissertation assessing the probable location of submerged archeological sites on the continental shelf stretching between Siberia and Alaska beneath the Bering Sea.

If the hypothesis was correct, the oldest archeological sites in the New World would be located in Alaska, and it was obviously just a matter of time until they were discovered. From the 1960s into the 1980s, archeologists, geologists, and paleontologists initiated major efforts to locate and document these early sites. During this period numerous caves were located and excavated, Pleistocene-age river terraces and sand dunes were surveyed and tested for archeological remains, fossil shorelines of lakes were examined, and thick deposits of windblown silt, or loess, deposited during the Pleistocene were searched for evidence of former human activity. No matter how creative and persevering our efforts were, we could not find unequivocal evidence of humans in Alaska any older than the Clovis sites farther south.

During the 1970s national energy needs increased oil exploration on the continental shelves lying off Alaska's coast. The National Oceanic and Atmospheric Administration, the Bureau of Land Management, the U.S. Geological Survey, and other agencies sponsored major research programs in these relatively unknown regions. Considerable data were accumulated during this time, enabling Hopkins to revise his history of the Bering Land Bridge in 1979. In 1982 Hopkins, along with his coeditors John Matthews, Charles Schweger, and Stephen Young, published *The Paleoecology of Beringia.* New research results indicated that Asia and North

11

Chapter 1

America were separated for the last time by rising sea level about or shortly after 14,000 years ago, rather than 10,000 years ago as scientists had believed in 1967.

More recently a series of peat deposits recovered from sediment cores taken from the floor of the Chukchi Sea have been dated approximately 11,000 B.P. (Elias et al. 1992). Analysis of the insects and other fossils with the peats, indicate that they were formed when this area of the continental shelf was exposed as land and suggests that the land bridge may not have been severed for the last time until about 10,000 B.P.

* * * * * * *

As I boarded the aircraft for my flight to Washington, D.C., I reflected on this complex set of interrelated problems. As tired as I was from the previous night's spearfishing, I felt a sense of excitement and adventure. For the past several months I had been in contact with Thomas Loy, a researcher at the University of British Columbia, who had developed an amazing new method for analyzing artifacts (Loy 1983). Together we had decided to apply his new method to the fluted projectile points that had been found in eastern Beringia.

Several years before this, Loy had been in the process of analyzing a large series of stone artifacts for wear patterns to determine how they might have been used in the prehistoric past. He repeatedly noted residue adhering to their surfaces. These residues were not new to archeologists; probably all of us at one time or another had seen them. Most of us considered them either interesting curiosities or obstructions that required vigorous cleaning so that we might more clearly view the "original" artifact. Loy, however, recognized them as something potentially significant. Through meticulous research he was able to determine that these residues were primarily blood. Carrying his idea further, he extracted some of the residue from the stone artifacts and began experimenting.

Through the addition of specific salts in specific concentrations, Loy forced the growth of hemoglobin crystals from the dried blood. Each species' hemoglobin will form a distinctive crystal, which is shared commonly by all other members of the species but not with any other species. Thus, one can identify the type of animal from which the blood on the artifact was derived. To do this one must have comparative data on the type of hemoglobin crystal that is characteristic of a particular species. If documented comparative information is not available or is inadequate, the crystals can be grown with little difficulty from a small blood sample taken from a living animal.

It was one thing to apply Loy's technique to relatively recent stone artifacts, but quite another to apply it to a group of artifacts that were believed to have been used to hunt extinct animals. If the residues on the fluted projectile points from eastern Beringia were derived from animals that are still alive today, there would be little problem identifying them. But what if they were not? How would we know what a mammoth hemoglobin crystal looked like even if we saw one? How could we obtain the blood of animals that had probably been extinct for more than 10,000 years? We had some ideas and were about to give them a try.

CHAPTER 2

PALEOINDIANS

 As one soars across the North American continent at forty thousand feet, one develops a deep respect for the first humans who colonized this vast continent. Its immense plains, powerful rivers, and rugged mountains, all inhabited by strange animals and plants, must have presented many challenges and perils. To learn to survive and prosper in the many new environments required ingenuity, strength, and determination. This was certainly one of the greatest challenges of the human experience.

The colonization of the Americas represents the last major dispersal of the human species on this planet. Within the sediments of the continent lies buried the evidence that documents this great event. The New World provides a fossil laboratory in which scientists study the role of our species dispersing over what were two relatively pristine continents. Understanding the response to this expansion of both the human population and the larger environment is important not only to biologists, anthropologists, and paleontologists but to all of humankind. It is important because we must not only understand ourselves from a historical perspective but also understand the incredible ability, or inability, of our species to initiate massive and irreversible change.

A major purpose of my trip to Washington, D.C., was to borrow from the Smithsonian Institution several of the fluted projectile points that had been found in eastern Beringia.

The specimens were from northern Alaska and included the original fluted point discovered by R. M. Thompson 40 years earlier. These artifacts, together with similar specimens from the University of Alaska Museum and the National Museum of Man in Canada, constituted virtually the entire assemblage of northern fluted points. Our goal was to examine as many of these specimens as possible for blood residues and thus avoid the biases that can occur if only a small number are examined. All of the specimens housed at the

Chapter 2

2.1 Examples of fluted projectile points from eastern Beringia.

Smithsonian were from Alaska's North Slope, a broad plain gradually sloping from the Brooks Range northward to the Arctic Ocean.

Because fluted projectile points represent the earliest widely accepted evidence for human populations in the Americas, the relationship of the specimens from eastern Beringia to those farther south is important to archeologists. Most researchers have assumed a historical relationship between the northern and southern examples. Their morphological similarity suggests that the fluted point assemblages in North America belong to a single, widespread tradition of toolmaking. In the southwestern United States, these artifacts are lumped together into what is called the Llano complex, which is comprised of Clovis (11,500–11,000 B.P.) artifacts, which are associated with mammoth remains, and Folsom (11,000–10,000 B.P.) artifacts, which are associated with the remains of extinct bison (Haynes 1964:1410). The Llano complex, in turn, is lumped into a large group of archeological remains that also includes younger

Paleoindians

artifact assemblages characterized by projectile points similar in form but lacking the diagnostic flutes. These artifacts were used to hunt and process extinct forms of bison and other large mammals. This larger group of artifacts, which includes the fluted projectile point assemblages, is referred to as the Paleoindian tradition. For the sake of clarity, I refer to similar artifacts from eastern Beringia as the Northern Paleoindian tradition.

Archeologists use the term tradition to describe groups of artifacts that are similar over a large geographic area and persist for long periods of time. The concept of an archeological tradition implies that a common way of life and economic pattern was passed from generation to generation throughout long periods during prehistoric times. Don Dumond, who has conducted extensive archeological field research in Alaska, has stressed that the beginning and end of a tradition is marked not only by major change in the types of artifacts used by the prehistoric peoples but also by a change in their economy (1982:39).

When people dramatically change the way they make and use tools and the economic system upon which their lives are based, one tradition comes to an end and a new one begins. For example, in the United States of America one way of life came to an end and another began with the industrial revolution. Many Americans are the direct descendents of late Iron Age agriculturalists who migrated to the Americas from Europe, but the tools and economic system in use today are dramatically different from those of their ancestors. These immigrants would feel as uncomfortable in our world as contemporary Americans would in theirs. Thus, we would consider the Iron Age a tradition different from the tradition of the Industrial Revolution, even though the people employing these traditions were genetically and culturally linked.

Traditions can change by other means as well. Some groups of people were overwhelmed by others, and their technological, social, and economic systems were dramatically and irreversibly changed. In some tragic cases entire human populations have been exterminated or displaced by other peoples. An example is the expansion of Euro-American culture at the expense of Native American cultures throughout the Americas. From an archeological perspective

Chapter 2

a dramatic change in technology and economy is documented by the tangible evidence in the form of artifacts and cultural features preserved within the earth across the American continents. These archeological sites provide mute testimony to the often cruel and brutal displacement of Native Americans by Euro-Americans. In this case Native American traditions came to an end not by progressive change from within, as occurred during the Industrial Revolution, but by the displacement of one human group by another.

A third method by which a tradition may come to an end is through assimilation. In this case one group of people gradually adopts the technological, social, and economic system of another until the two are essentially indistinguishable from each other. Many populations immigrating to the United States, either voluntarily or not, have abandoned their language, technology, and social and economic systems to become integrated into American culture. Except for obvious genetically inherited traits such as skin and eye color, they are indistinguishable from the rest of the population.

Thus, when we speak of the Northern Paleoindian tradition we make an underlying assumption that the peoples who made and used fluted projectile points in eastern Beringia were part of a larger population of peoples who shared a similar way of life and economic system. There are fundamentally three hypotheses (Clark 1984) that have been advanced to explain the similarities between the northern and southern Paleoindian assemblages. The first suggests that the northern specimens were left by the first humans to reach Alaska, who subsequently spread southward from eastern Beringia to colonize the continents. If this proposition is true, the northern artifacts must necessarily be older than the southern ones. It would also be expected that similar, and even older, examples of these artifacts would be found in western Beringia.

The second hypothesis proposes that fluted projectile points developed in the more southern regions of North America and spread northward into eastern Beringia. To prove this theory, the southern examples must necessarily be older than their northern counterparts. It also requires that even older archeological remains must exist from which the later distinctive fluted point technology

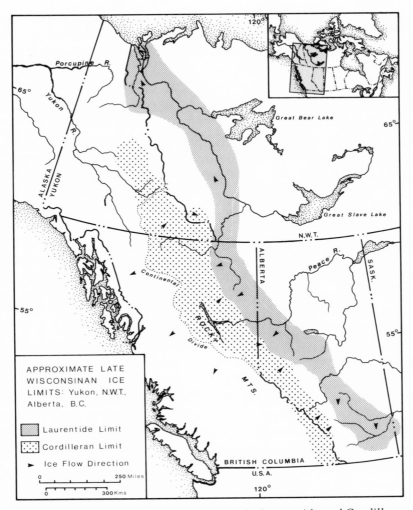

2.2 *Approximate late Wisconsin ice limits of the Laurentide and Cordilleran glaciers in the area of western Canada (compiled from Rutter 1984, Clague et al. 1989).*

developed. The third hypothesis suggests that fluted points were independently invented in eastern Beringia thousands of years after those to the south and that there may be no historical relationship between the two groups of artifacts.

Chapter 2

The proof of these hypotheses lies in establishing the age of the fluted points. Though this has been accomplished in the south, northern fluted points have not been dated. All the northern fluted points have been recovered either as isolated surface finds lacking preserved bone and adequate geological context or from sites where radiocarbon or other dating techniques have yielded ambiguous age determinations.

Critical to understanding the potential relationships between these artifact assemblages is the presence or absence of an ice free corridor leading from eastern Beringia to the interior of the North American continent.

During the last glacial (the Wisconsin), an enormous glacier called the Laurentide ice sheet, formed in eastern Canada. Concurrently, glaciers in the Canadian Rockies in the west began to flow out of the mountains; they coalesced and spread eastward, forming another massive ice sheet called the Cordilleran. These massive glaciers expanded until they met in the area that is today Alberta and northern British Columbia, Canada.

The merged Cordilleran and Laurentide ice would have formed an impenetrable barrier stretching from the Atlantic Ocean to the Pacific Ocean and more than 500 miles from eastern Beringia to southern Alberta. For human groups who survived on an economy based on hunting, gathering, and fishing, the massive continental glacier would have presented a lifeless, dangerous, seemingly endless ice-scape. Archeologists agree that the merged continental glaciers would have formed a barrier so severe that it would have been impossible for humans to cross it during the late Pleistocene.

The concept of an ice-free corridor stretching between eastern Beringia and the unglaciated southern areas of North America was first suggested by W. A. Johnston in 1933, when he outlined the extent of continental glaciation and mechanisms that created the Bering Land Bridge. The term ice-free corridor is applied to a relatively narrow strip of unglaciated land between the Laurentide and Cordilleran ice. Although many researchers agree that these two ice sheets joined in western Canada, some suggest that this was a very brief event and that the ice soon withdrew, leaving a relatively narrow strip of unglaciated land between these huge glaciers. They

Paleoindians

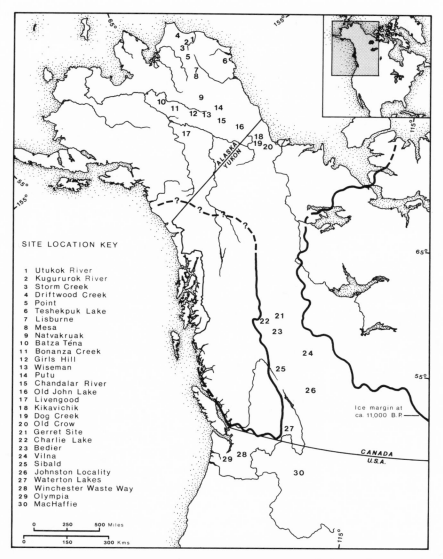

SITE LOCATION KEY

1 Utukok River
2 Kugururok River
3 Storm Creek
4 Driftwood Creek
5 Point
6 Teshekpuk Lake
7 Lisburne
8 Mesa
9 Natvakruak
10 Batza Téna
11 Bonanza Creek
12 Girls Hill
13 Wiseman
14 Putu
15 Chandalar River
16 Old John Lake
17 Livengood
18 Kikavichik
19 Dog Creek
20 Old Crow
21 Gerret Site
22 Charlie Lake
23 Bedier
24 Vilna
25 Sibald
26 Johnston Locality
27 Waterton Lakes
28 Winchester Waste Way
29 Olympia
30 MacHaffie

2.3 The distribution of fluted projectile point sites in relation to the retreating continential ice (ca. 11,000 B.P.).

Chapter 2

further theorize that this narrow corridor would have provided an avenue through which plants, animals, and humans could have passed from Beringia into other unglaciated regions of North America. Other species could have moved from south to north through the corridor. It should be stressed that the existence of an ice-free corridor has not been satisfactorily proved by researchers working in the area. Canadian paleoecologist Glen MacDonald (1987b) demonstrated that some of the most important radiocarbon dates used to support the existence of an ice-free corridor are in error. He persuasively (MacDonald 1987a,b) argues that an ice-free corridor never existed until the end of the Wisconsin, when the continental ice began its final retreat.

The Wisconsin geology in the area of Canada critical to the discussion of an ice-free corridor is extremely complex. It may be many years before adequate field data are available to resolve satisfactorily this difficult problem. However, the ice did coalesce in some areas during the late Wisconsin. Even if isolated pockets of unglaciated terrain persisted amidst a sea of ice, such areas probably would have been biotically impoverished. In these restricted environments, if they existed at all, humans would have found it difficult to survive until deglaciation was sufficiently advanced to support adequate resources in the form of plants and animals essential to sustain groups of hunters and gatherers.

By 11,000 years ago the continental glaciers had withdrawn sufficiently to create a wide corridor extending from eastern Beringia to interior North America (Rutter 1984, Clague et al. 1989). Several sites that contain fluted projectile points have been reported in this region. All of these sites have been found outside the limits of the continental ice as it existed approximately 11,000 years ago. This suggests these sites may have been occupied sometime between the beginning of deglaciation (Prest 1984, Haynes 1987:84), probably between 12,000–13,000 years ago, and 11,000 years ago. This information is only suggestive because sites within this ice-free area could have been occupied at anytime following deglaciation. Sites occurring in the area glaciated 11,000 years ago would necessarily be more recent than that. Advancing glaciers likely would have destroyed sites which predated glaciation, if such sites existed at all.

Paleoindians

Another persuasive argument supporting the relationship of the northern and southern fluted projectile point sites is their geographic distribution. If the Northern Paleoindian tradition developed independently and later than the Llano complex, a geographic gap, or hiatus might exist between the two groups of sites. Continued field research during the past two decades has reduced the geographic hiatus between the northern and southern groups of sites. With the exception of a relatively small area in the southeastern portion of the Yukon Territory, sites are continuously distributed from the northern plains of the United States to Alaska. Although future fieldwork will continue to fill in this picture, we now have enough information to recognize that the distribution of these sites is continuous throughout Canada's ice-free corridor, providing the essential geographic link between the north and south.

In terms of considering these sites as representative of a single, widespread cultural tradition, two of the three major criteria have been met. First, their morphological similarity was recognized soon after the first eastern Beringian examples were discovered, and subsequent discoveries have strengthened these observations. Second, field research in recent years has demonstrated that these sites were part of a large and continuous geographic distribution. The remaining unanswered question is whether the peoples who occupied these archeological sites thousands of years ago shared a similar economic system based, at least to a large degree, on hunting mammoth and other extinct Pleistocene animals.

* * * * * * *

With the help of my colleagues at the Smithsonian Institution I had located the fluted projectile points from eastern Beringia. My short stay in Washington, D.C., had been hectic. Between meetings with staff of the National Science Foundation and the National Geographic Society, the specimens were carefully packed and the required loan and insurance forms were signed. As I closely examined the artifacts before packing them, I thought I could

Chapter 2

recognize minute amounts of residue preserved in very small cracks and crevices on the surface of some of the artifacts. This was encouraging because these specimens had been subject to repeated analysis and cleaning over the years.

I boarded the airplane to New York City with a sense of mounting excitement. As the plane flew along the populated eastern seaboard of North America, I reflected on what I expected to find upon analyzing the preserved residues. Based on circumstantial evidence, I reasoned that the Northern Paleoindian tradition sites represented a backwash of Paleoindian hunters who entered the region from the south pursuing the remnants of Pleistocene bison sometime after mammoth had become extinct in the north. I anticipated that we would find the blood of modern bison and other contemporary species on the points. This hypothesis had been untestable before Tom Loy had developed his innovative technique, but now it was within the realm of possibility to objectively test this idea.

CHAPTER 3
FEAST OR FAMINE IN BERINGIA

It had rained during the night and the grass outside New York's American Museum of Natural History was wet. As I waited outside the museum for Gary Selinger, a colleague from the University of Alaska Museum, to join me, I reflected on my home institution. It occupies a building specifically designed and constructed to house the University of Alaska's scientific research collections. The museum building is named after one of Alaska's pioneer natural historians, Otto William Geist. Geist was a largely self-educated scholar with a passion for collecting plants, animals, artifacts, and fossils. His collections formed the nucleus of the University of Alaska Museum. He worked in collaboration with and with support from the University's first president, Charles Bunnell.

During the 1920s and 1930s, when Geist was most active, gold mining was a major industry in the area of Fairbanks, Alaska. Huge dredges floated in artificial ponds mining the gold-bearing gravels buried deep within the valley bottoms. The dredges moved by slowly excavating the areas ahead of them, causing their artificial ponds to advance. Debris, or tailings, were deposited behind the dredges thus filling the lake behind them. Alaska Natives humorously referred to the dredges as the world's slowest boats!

For the dredges to reach the deep gold-bearing gravels, massive deposits of frozen Pleistocene organic silt, loess, and peat, which the miners called muck, were removed by thawing the ground and washing the muck away with hydraulic hoses. As this overburden was removed the miners made spectacular discoveries. In some cases the silt had been frozen shortly after it was deposited and remained frozen until thawed and exposed by the miners. These deposits contained the bones, teeth, and tusks of thousands of animals that had died during the Pleistocene. Some animals had been preserved with flesh, hide, and even hair intact!

These important discoveries did not escape the attention of a man with Geist's passion for collecting. With financial support from

25

Chapter 3

wealthy paleontologist Charles Frick at the American Museum of Natural History in New York, Geist began collecting thousands of specimens from the muck deposits. These specimens were carefully packed and shipped to the American Museum of Natural History. Among the more spectacular finds were the foot of a mammoth calf, another mammoth calf with the face, trunk, and one front leg intact, a nearly complete Pleistocene moose, numerous legs of Pleistocene horse and bison, and the complete mummified carcasses of many small mammals.

3.1 Abandoned gold dredge, Fish Creek, Alaska.

Walter and Ruth Roman and their sons discovered the virtually complete carcass of an extinct bison *(Bison priscus)* while removing overburden at their gold mine in interior Alaska. Paleontologists from the University of Alaska, Dale and Mary Lee Guthrie, excavated the bison and discovered that it was so well preserved that the animal could be restored for display much the same way taxidermists mount large trophy animals. Because of the concentration of vivianite, a blue mineral, surrounding the carcass, Guthrie named the fossil Blue Babe

Feast or Famine

3.2 Mummified face and left foreleg of a mammoth calf, American Museum of Natural History, New York.

3.3 Mummified foot of a mammoth calf, American Museum of Natural History, New York.

Chapter 3

after Paul Bunyan's blue ox (Guthrie 1988). To the delight of thousands of visitors, Blue Babe is now on display at the University of Alaska Museum just as it was encapsulated in the earth some 36,000 years ago.

The nature of the environment and climate in which these animals lived has been the subject of speculation for many years. Dale Guthrie (1968, 1982, 1990) has suggested that because many of these animals (such as the extinct horse, bison, and mammoth) were grazers, the environment must have been composed primarily of grasses. Others (Cwynar and Ritchie 1980, Ritchie 1984, and Ritchie and Cwynar 1982) have argued that the animals may have lived in eastern Beringia during the warmer interglacials and that the environment at the close of the Pleistocene was severe—characterized by high winds and very little vegetation. Massive sand dunes dating to the very late Pleistocene have been documented (Hopkins 1982) over vast areas of eastern Beringia. Because vegetation stabilizes the soil and prevents it from blowing away, the dunes indicate not only high winds but very little vegetation. On one hand researchers find evidence for a severe and biotically impoverished environment, and on the other they find fossil evidence suggesting that the environment supported large numbers of very large animals with more mammalian species present than survive in eastern Beringia today. These two seemingly opposing sets of evidence have been called the productivity paradox.

The problem is important to prehistorians because if the Beringian environment was so impoverished during the late Pleistocene that it could not support human populations, then colonization of the Americas via the Bering Land Bridge may not have been possible. Because of the disturbed situation in which the remains of many of the extinct animals were found during the course of stripping the overburden during mining, it is very difficult to tell whether these animals lived together at approximately the same time or lived during different times, possibly in different environments. The major question asked by paleoecologists is whether the fossils recovered from the numerous Pleistocene exposures represent biocenoses, i.e., mammalian communities that lived together at the same time. Another critical question is when these animals became extinct. If mammoth, for example, became extinct before the first humans arrived in eastern Beringia, then a critical link is missing from the chain of reasoning that suggests that these first humans were mammoth hunters who spread from western to eastern Beringia and then southward into the rest of North and South America.

The youngest dates for any given species or genus establish what geologists and archeologists call minimum limiting dates. In other words, researchers realize that it is extremely unlikely that the bone they have dated is from the very last surviving animal of a species that became extinct. Consequently, they consider the youngest date for any given species as a minimum limiting date, which indicates that the species most probably became extinct sometime after the most recent date available. If a new and younger date becomes available, it then becomes the minimum limiting date for that species.

There are two ways to determine the time during which the animals lived. One method is to determine the nature and age of the geologic deposit from which it came, and the other is to date the carbon in the bone itself. During the past decade an increasing number of radiocarbon dates have been run directly on the bones of Pleistocene fauna from eastern Beringia. In a few cases, bones have been found in geologic deposits that have been accurately dated. These dates not only document when the animals lived, but when compiled together, demonstrate the length of time animals inhabited the region.

Hopkins (1982) has subdivided the last major glaciation, the Wisconsin, into four distinct regional episodes: 1) the Happy interval (older than 60,000 to 80,000 years ago), 2) the Boutellier interval (60,000 to 80,000–30,000 years ago), 3) the Duvanny Yar interval (30,000–14,000 years ago), and 4) the Birch interval (14,000–8,500 years ago). With the exception of the Birch interval, which is named for the rise of birch in the pollen record during that time, each period is named after a locality where geologic deposits have been found and analyzed, providing insights to the environment during that time. Of particular interest to archeologists are the Duvanny Yar and Birch intervals, the periods in which most researchers believe humans first entered the Americas.

Two species are particularly important in assessing the environ-

Chapter 3

ment of eastern Beringia during the time when it is likely that humans spread into the Americas: mammoth and bison. These two types of animals are most commonly associated with Paleoindian sites that have been excavated south of the former continental ice, dating from the close of the Pleistocene. Although there are numerous radiocarbon dates for these species throughout the late Pleistocene, it is most important for archeologists to test the productivity paradox for the past 16,000 years (the end of the Duvanny Yar to present), since this time is considered most likely for humans to have entered the New World via the Bering Land Bridge. If these species were not present in eastern Beringia at the close of the Pleistocene, then large mammal hunters spreading eastward from western Beringia across the Bering Land Bridge would have found eastern Beringia a barren, hostile environment. Perhaps it was even an impenetrable barrier to colonizing the Americas.

Some of the initial pollen data suggested that eastern Beringia was characterized by a sparse vegetation similar to that of the high arctic today (Colinvaux 1964, 1986; Colinvaux and West 1984; Cwynar 1982; Ritchie and Cwynar 1982), which could not support the diverse megafauna assemblage seen in the paleontological record. However, more recent pollen data from a lowland setting in western Alaska in the Kotzebue Sound area indicate that during the full glacial there was meadow-like tundra dominated by grasses and sedges (Anderson 1985), vegetation types similar to the composition of stomach contents of large mammal mummies found in western Beringia (Ukraintseva 1985).

A dynamic Canadian paleoecologist, Charles Schweger (1982), has proposed what is probably a more realistic concept of the late Pleistocene environment of eastern Beringia, more realistic because it reconciles the seemingly conflicting fossil floral and faunal records. He proposes that the environment was actually a complex mosaic of wetland meadows and ponds on the river floodplains with mixed grasslands and tundra occupying river terraces. He postulates that tundra existed on the pediments and foothills of the mountain ranges and that the mountains were unvegetated. His view of the late Pleistocene environment of eastern Beringia provides diverse environmental zones depending on elevation, moisture, and topography, which would provide the types of vegetation necessary to support the great variety of Wisconsin age herbivores.

3.4 Dima, a complete mammoth calf discovered in 1977 in the Kolyma area, northeast Siberia (courtesy of the USSR Academy of Science, Magadan).

Other researchers (P. J. Martin 1982, Redman 1982) have stressed the importance of the animal community in modifying and maintaining the environment through selectively feeding on certain types or parts of plants and through manure and urea deposition and carcass decay. More recently a South African paleoecologist,

Chapter 3

Norman Owen-Smith (1987) has studied the habits of the large African herbivores and their important roles in modifying the environment in a variety of ways that create favorable habitat for smaller mammals. He argues that with the extinction of the large herbivores the habitat changed dramatically, thus contributing to the extinction of many smaller herbivores dependent on the environment created and maintained by the larger animals.

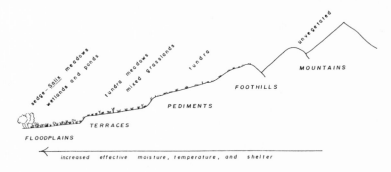

3.5 Proposed late Wisconsin vegetation continuum from lowlands to mountains for eastern Beringia. (Schweger 1982:111, reproduced with permission from Academic Press and the author.)

Although there are few radiocarbon dates from eastern Beringia for mammoth (figure 3.6) at the close of the Pleistocene, the available dates strongly suggest that this species persisted in eastern Beringia well into the Birch interval. This supports Schweger's view of the environment of eastern Beringia because the mere presence of mammoth indicates that suitable habitat existed in at least some areas to support them. The most recent radiocarbon dates suggest a minimum limiting date for mammoth extinction at some time more recent than 11,000 years ago.   As additional dates become available, the limiting date could become younger. The fact that mammoth probably persisted until at least 11,000 years ago is significant because firmly documented archeological sites in Alaska are also that old. This suggests that humans and mammoth were contemporaneous in eastern Beringia; however, we have not found mammoth kill sites in the north like the sites farther south.

Feast or Famine

Late Radiocarbon Dates for Mammoth

Eastern Beringia

Date	Lab. No.	Locality	Reference
15,550 ± 130	GSC-3053	Bluefish Cave, Yukon Territory	Guthrie 1985
15,380 ± 300	SI-453	Fairbanks Creek, Alaska	Pewe 1975
15,280 ± 120	[1]BETA-16996	Colorado Creek, Alaska	Unpubl. data, on file, UA Museum
15,090 ± 170	BETA-5691	Colorado Creek, Alaska	Guthrie 1985
14,270 ± 950	BETA-20027	Trail Creek, Alaska	Schaaf 1988
13,340 ± 115	DIC-2130	Teklanika River, Alaska	Guthrie 1985
12,980 ± 250	[1]BETA-9906	Colorado Creek, Alaska	Guthrie 1985
12,622 ± 750	W-401	Fairbanks, Alaska	Hester 1960
11,360 ± 100	BETA-13811	Trail Creek Caves, Alaska	Vinson 1988
10,050 ± 150	I-9998	Lost Chicken Creek, Alaska	Harrington 1978

[1] Same bone

3.6 Late radicarbon dates for mammoth, eastern Beringia.

There were no bison in Alaska when the first Europeans and Americans began to explore the area. Furthermore, no records suggest that Alaska Natives remembered bison in the region. This suggests that bison became extinct well before the early 1700s. The most recent radiocarbon date, from Chester Creek, seems anomalous; possibly it is the misidentified remains of a domestic cow or bull introduced by Russian explorers or fur traders, or simply an inaccurate radiocarbon date

The radiocarbon dates for bison (figure 3.7) in eastern Beringia demonstrate that they did not become extinct at the end of the Pleistocene but rather persisted throughout much of the Holocene. Extinct bison were likely part of a larger population of bison known as wood bison, whose range is now restricted to Wood Buffalo National Park south of Canada's Great Slave Lake. These large game animals must have played an important role in the subsistence economy of humans inhabiting the region. However, as in the case of mammoth, well-defined bison kill sites similar to those farther

Chapter 3

Late Radiocarbon Dates for Bison

Eastern Beringia

Date	Lab No.	Location	Reference
13,070 ± 280	K-1327	Trail Creek Cave 9, Alaska	Larsen 1968
12,460 ± 320	SI-290	Cleary Creek, Alaska	Pewe 1975
12,460 ± 220	I-3574	Old Crow, Locality 11, Yukon Territory	Harrington 1978
12,275 ± 180	I-7764	Old Crow, Locality 11, Yukon Territory	Harrington 1978
11,980 ± 135	ST-1633	Fairbanks Creek, Alaska	Harrington 1978
11,910 ± 180	I-7765	Old Crow, Locality 11, Yukon Territory	Harrington 1978
11,735 ± 130	ST-1631	Cleary Creek, Alaska	Pewe 1975
10,715 ± 225	SI-1561	Dry Creek, Alaska	Guthrie 1985
10,370 ± 160	I-8582	Lost Chicken Creek, Alaska	Harrington 1980
9,000 ± 250	BETA-18552	Arch Cave, Porcupine River, Alaska	Unpubl. data on file, UAF Museum
7,195 ± 100	SI-1117	Canyon Site, Yukon, Canada	Harrington 1978
6,730 ± 260	W-1108	Sullivan Pit, Alaska	Repenning et al. 1964
5,340 ± 110	SI-845	Goldstream area, Fairbanks, Alaska	Pewe 1975
2,285 ± 145	GX-6750	Central, Alaska	Holmes and Bacon 1982
1,350 ± 95	I-5404	Dawson, Locality 6, Yukon Territory	Harrington 1977
470 ± 90	SI-852	Chester Creek Bridge, Anchorage, AK	Guthrie 1990

3.7 Late radiocarbon dates for bison, eastern Beringia.

south have not been discovered in eastern Beringia, although a few identifiable bison remains have been found in archeological sites.

American archeologists have relied heavily on what is called the direct historic approach in attempting to locate archeological sites. Through the literature and historic accounts describing Native American cultures and economic systems, they search for former habitation sites in areas that were used by prehistoric peoples for various activities. For example, if the peoples in a region were known to fish at the outlet of lakes at the time of contact with Euro-American cultures, then archeologists will look for archeological sites in those types of ecological settings.

This approach has two major problems. One is that by the time

Feast or Famine

most Native Americans came into direct contact with Euro-Americans, their economies and cultures had already changed as a result of prior indirect contact. For example, both trade goods and disease reached most Native American groups well before they saw Euro-Americans. A dramatic example is the introduction of the horse into the New World by the Spaniards. Within a matter of a few centuries this led to the development of the elaborate equestrian bison-hunting cultures of the North American plains. People who had been sedentary farmers along the river valleys abandoned their old way of life to become what is for many contemporary North Americans a stereotype of Native American culture.

The second major problem with the direct historic approach is that it does not take into account the many significant changes in the environment that led to major changes in the quantity and types of resources available to peoples whose economy was based on hunting and gathering. These changes in the environment profoundly affected the distribution and kinds of resources upon which their economy was based. This in turn necessitated shifts in the settlement patterns to exploit them.

Archeologists working in eastern Beringia are perhaps more prone to adopt the direct historic approach than are others. Numerous Native American groups still live throughout Alaska and northwest Canada. Because direct contact between Native Americans and Euro-Americans was comparatively late in this region, Native American cultures and economic systems were relatively well recorded. Through conversations with Athapaskans of the interior and by reading their literature one can readily discover that fish and caribou were the primary faunal resources in the early economy of these people. Thus, archeologists have searched for archeological sites at excellent fishing and caribou hunting areas. Though this approach is effective for finding archeological sites dating to historic and late prehistoric times, it completely overlooks earlier archeological sites such as those associated with bison predation which occurred more than a thousand years ago.

One of the great ironies concerning the archeology of the noncoastal areas of eastern Beringia is that the carcasses of Pleistocene mammals are exceptionally well preserved, occasionally

Chapter 3

with hide, hair, and even flesh intact, while only a very few organic artifacts more than 1,000 years old have been preserved. This has necessitated an interpretation of the prehistory based largely upon the stone artifacts alone, since the bones from most of these archeological sites have decomposed and thus leave little evidence from which to interpret the basis of the economy or environmental change. However, blood residue analysis might provide a heretofore unrecognized opportunity to address these problems by permitting species identification in the absence of other faunal remains.

* * * * * * *

When Gary Selinger arrived outside the American Museum of Natural History, we exchanged greetings and eagerly entered the building, in which lay the carcasses of the preserved Pleistocene mammals recovered 50 years earlier by Geist and shipped to New York. Richard Tedford, the curator at the American Museum in charge of these rare finds, graciously had given us permission to collect tissue samples from these animals. We had come prepared with vials, scalpels, and surgical gloves with which to carefully remove and store the tissue. My hope was that the muscle tissue would contain enough blood so that it could be extracted and hemoglobin crystals could be grown from it. Because the carcasses were fairly complete, there was no ambiguity in identifying the animals from which the dried blood was derived.

Although all these specimens originally had been preserved by freezing, the muscle was very different from the comparatively fresh meat one encounters in a supermarket. All of the samples were extremely dry. Over the millennia moisture had escaped from the tissue, a process more like freeze-drying than just freezing. Additional moisture had escaped from the tissues since the time of their excavation. As a result, the remains were a sinuous and extremely resilient mass of intertwined tissue similar to beef jerky, which was covered by hide more like iron than leather. The tissue was so tough that it could only be cut with great difficulty with a scalpel or heavy, sharp scissors. As we worried our way though the remains of one

Feast or Famine

3.8 The author (left) and Gary Selinger (right) collecting fossil tissue samples at the American Museum of Natural History.

prehistoric beast after another, we carefully recorded from where and what type of animal each sample was collected. Each was carefully stored in an individual sample vial and each vial was labeled.

The preservation was excellent. My hopes were high that from these samples we would be able to force the first growth of hemoglobin crystals from extinct animals.

CHAPTER 4
ARTIFACT OR PSEUDOFACT

 During the course of our work collecting the tissue samples we also read the well-organized files at the American Museum, which provided the supporting documentation associated with the fossils. It was exciting to read the original letters from Charles Bunnell describing Geist's field collecting and itemizing the expenses incurred. Gary and I chuckled at the cost of doing fieldwork during the 1930s. Compared to today's prices everything seemed ridiculously cheap. Charles Frick had obviously gotten his money's worth. The results constituted an important legacy for the future.

One letter in particular caught my interest. Bunnell described uniquely modified antlers that had come from the muck deposits, which he illustrated with an enclosed photo. He was sure the antlers had been modified by humans and expressed his belief that these specimens, along with other modified bones, were important evidence of human occupation of eastern Beringia during the Pleistocene. I was intimately familiar with the specimens illustrated in the photo because I had rediscovered them in the University of Alaska Museum's collection and actually had published a picture of them ten years earlier (Dixon 1976). In my opinion they had not been modified by humans. After analyzing the antlers, I concluded that they had acquired their unique configurations through the gnawing and chewing of animals and that they had been selectively culled from the large quantities of bone and other material from the muck deposits. This difference of opinion lay at the heart of one of the most controversial issues in Pleistocene archeology during the 1970s and 1980s.

The fundamental question is simple: Under what conditions can modification of osseous material (bone, antler, and ivory) be attributed to human activity? As with many scientific endeavors, the question may be simple, but the answers are complex. In this case, the answers are so complex that they have led archeologists

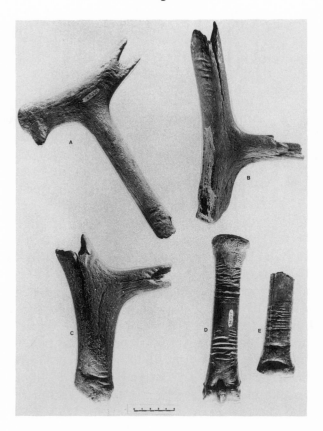

4.1 Gnawed Pleistocene antlers (a, b, c,) and gnawed bone (d, e) recovered from the Fairbanks muck deposits.

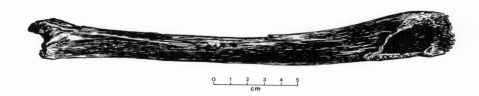

4.2 Caribou tibia flesher from the Old Crow area, Yukon Territory (redrawn from Bonnichsen 1979:161 and Morlan 1980:128).

Artifact or Pseudofact

and paleontologists into an entirely new field of research called taphonomy. Taphonomy has been defined as the study of processes acting on organisms from the time of their death to the time of their discovery as fossils (Behrensmeyer and Hill 1980). However, I prefer a broader definition that encompasses modifications that may occur while an animal is still alive. This definition is important because bones, antlers, and tusks can be broken, polished, and otherwise modified during the life of the animal. When the animal subsequently dies, these modified bones become incorporated in the fossil record. Perhaps a more suitable definition for archeologically related taphonomic studies is "the study of the physical, biological, and cultural processes which result in the modification of mammalian remains, especially bones, including the process of preservation and destruction as fossils" (Dixon and Thorson 1984:155).

Taphonomy is extremely important to the question of the first arrival of humans into the Americas. Virtually all of the evidence supporting human occupation of eastern Beringia when the Bering Land Bridge existed is taphonomic. Bunnell's letter and an archeological report by Helge Larsen (1968a) discussing his 1949 cave excavation on Alaska's Seward Peninsula foreshadowed this debate.

In 1966 a Canadian scientist, C. R. Harington, working near the Athapaskan village of Old Crow in Canada's Yukon Territory, discovered a bone tool virtually identical to those used today to remove the excess flesh and fat from the inner side of animal hides. When he and archeologist William Irving reported radiocarbon-dating this caribou bone flesher to approximately 27,000 years ago (Irving and Harington 1973), the debate became increasingly heated. For years paleontologists had been collecting bones from extinct Pleistocene species along the banks of the Porcupine and Old Crow rivers in Canada's Yukon Territory. In the process they collected several bone artifacts that were stained in the same manner as were the Pleistocene bones. The artifacts were made from the bones of caribou and other species that may have lived either in Pleistocene times or more recently. Irving and Harington reasoned that the process of staining took a very long time and suggested that the Pleistocene bones and the artifacts might be of the same age. In addition to the artifacts, these collections contained vast quantities

41

of spirally fractured, flaked, polished, cut, striated, and faceted bone. Upon examining these specimens, Irving, along with his students and colleagues, suspected that the bones may have been modified by humans. They suggested that these bones and the few associated artifacts represented tangible evidence of what were probably the earliest humans to occupy eastern Beringia. The collective weight of these finds suggested to several archeologists that human hunters had reached North America by at least 27,000 years ago, and some researchers (Jopling et al. 1981) postulated much earlier dates. Unfortunately, none of these artifacts were from true archeological sites, and most were recovered along sand and gravel bars where they had been deposited or exposed by the Old Crow and Porcupine rivers.

Robson Bonnichsen (1979) undertook an elaborate and in-depth series of replicative experiments in which he flaked and fractured bones. He produced bone flakes and the larger pieces of bone from which they had been struck, called cores, and observed that they were virtually identical to the specimens found through-out the Old Crow basin. The results led him to conclude that much of the flaking and modification of Pleistocene bones had been done by humans. Fresh, or green, bone fractures spirally when broken; fossil bone tends not to. Many of the Pleistocene bones in the collection exhibited spiral fractures, indicating that they were broken or modified soon after the animal died, thus establishing the time at which the bone was modified.

The long bones of large mammals contain marrow, which is not only delicious but was highly valued by contemporary and prehis-toric hunters as a source of fat. Fractured marrow bones are among the most abundant remains encountered in many archeological sites. These bone fragments exhibit typical spiral green-bone fractures and occasional impact scars where they were struck by hammer-like objects to break them. Many of the Pleisto-cene bones found in the Old Crow area are virtually identical to marrow bones recovered from archeological sites. This led researchers to suspect that the bones were evidence of marrow extraction by Pleistocene hunters of these extinct animals.

The evidence continued to mount, and many researchers

Artifact or Pseudofact

were convinced that the few tools and the vast quantities of modified bone from the Yukon Territory documented the presence of human groups in North America during the Pleistocene. There were troubling problems with the nature of the evidence. For example, many archeologists believed that the stone tools should necessarily be associated with the bones, however, they were not. Were there other noncultural mechanisms that could fracture, flake, and modify bone to produce virtually identical characteristics? Could some of the tools have been made more recently from the bones of Pleistocene animals by prehistoric hunters who had found them much the same way scientists had? Most importantly, where were the archeological sites from which these artifacts had come?

Archeologist Dennis Stanford is a Smithsonian Institution curator who walks the streets of Washington, D.C., dressed in faded denims and cowboy boots. He is perhaps the leading expert in the Pleistocene archeology of the Americas, and he has outlined four tests to determine the age and validity of an archeological site or group of artifacts. Although some archeologists might argue that his criteria are too rigid, most would agree that they provide the scientific rigor necessary to demonstrate Pleistocene occupation of the Americas. He (Stanford 1979, 1983:65) suggests that the following questions should be asked of all archeological sites purported to date to the Pleistocene and used as evidence of early human occupation of the Americas:

1) Are the recovered artifacts clearly the product of human manufacture?
2) Is the recovered material in clear stratigraphic context?
3) Are there concurrent radiocarbon dates from the deposit?
4) Do paleoenvironmental studies support the chronological placement of the site?

For an archeological site to be accepted as evidence for Pleistocene human occupation of the Americas, it must pass not one, but all four of the above tests. In the absence of tools, human bones dated to the Pleistocene would also provide acceptable evidence.

When these criteria were applied to the artifacts and faunal remains recovered from the Old Crow region, it was apparent that there were major problems in assessing the significance of these finds. All of the artifacts and even a human skull had been recovered from areas where they had been redeposited by the Porcupine and Old Crow rivers. Consequently, it was impossible to assess their age based on their stratigraphic position and associated radiocarbon or other dates derived from geologic deposits.

One thing was clear: the Old Crow artifacts could be no older than the bones from which they were manufactured, the logical limit for the oldest possible date. However, radiocarbon-dating could determine only the age of the bone, not the time at which it was fashioned into a tool. The artifacts possibly could have been made more recently from the bones of Pleistocene mammals that had died thousands of years earlier. The fact that some of the artifacts were stained in much the same manner as the bones of extinct Pleistocene animals did not provide enough evidence to conclusively prove that they were the same age. Bones of domestic animals, such as cows and pigs, cut by metal saws and left by the early miners in the Fairbanks area have been recovered, and they are stained in the same manner as are Pleistocene bones recovered nearby.

Further complicating the problem is the fact that radiocarbon-dating is a destructive technique requiring that the organic material used for dating be burned to obtain an age determination. The method is reliable for samples as old as circa 40,000 years, and samples older than this are considered by many researchers to be minimum limiting ages. The older the sample, the more material must be sacrificed for dating. At the time Old Crow specimens were found, most, and in some cases all, of a given specimen would have to have been destroyed to obtain a reliable radiocarbon date. Some scientists suspected that some of the artifacts may have been older than the range of radiocarbon-dating. They feared that attempting to date them by the radiocarbon method might result in the loss of the original specimens and forever negate the possibility of determining the true age of the artifacts. A caribou bone flesher had already been largely sacrificed to obtain the radiocarbon date of 27,000 B.P. The researchers realized that the remaining specimens, which could possibly be the oldest artifacts ever found in the Americas, should not be destroyed.

Another facet of the problem was considerably more complex. Some of the modified bones were believed to result from marrow extraction by humans during the Pleistocene. Although not all had been found in primary depositional contexts, they were recovered in geologic deposits laid down tens of thousands of years ago as ancient lake sediments or in deposits of the Porcupine and Old Crow rivers. Archeologists exhibited little disagreement regarding the age of most of these bones but disputed whether they had been altered by humans. As a result, the difficulty of distinguishing between bones that had been modified by humans and those that had been modified by other means became important.

Not only is this problem important to researchers attempting to understand the timing of the peopling of the Americas, but it is also a thorny problem for archeologists attempting to evaluate the earliest evidence for human evolution in Africa and other areas of the Old World. For many years, modified bones from these areas of the world were interpreted to be possibly some of the first tools used or manufactured by the emerging primates destined to become our ancestors. Every professional meeting of any import included slides of archeologists flaking and fracturing the green bone of recently deceased zoo elephants and slides of archeologists up to their elbows in blood while butchering kangaroos or other animals with stone tools. Researchers conducted these experiments to find out what the osseous remains of large mammals looked like after being flaked, fractured, or butchered by humans using stone or bone tools. The evidence from these experiments were compared with evidence from alleged prehistoric sites.

While these experiments were in progress, another group of researchers began an exhaustive, painstaking examination of what osseous materials looked like after being subjected to a vast array of noncultural phenomena. This different research approach required the examination and documentation of carnivore and rodent gnawing of bone, trampling of bone by large mammals at watering holes, modification of bone by rockfall in caves, alteration of bone by the powerful movements of river ice, natural fracture of bone during the

Chapter 4

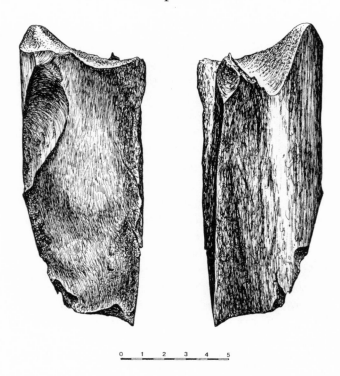

4.3 Spirally fractured and flaked bone core, University of Alaska Museum.

life of an animal, and a vast array of other physical, chemical, and biological processes that did not involve humans. Over time it became increasingly apparent that an infinite array of phenomena in various combinations and circumstances modify bones to be essentially indistinguishable from bones modified by humans.

For example, caribou are frequently drowned as they attempt to cross the Porcupine River in the spring when the river ice has broken up and is moving rapidly down the swollen river in massive chunks. I have talked to residents of the area who have seen animals with spirally fractured long bones protruding from their legs, injured while attempting this difficult crossing. Other animals have been observed trapped on ice floes moving rapidly down the river to face certain death. The bones of all these animals are ultimately

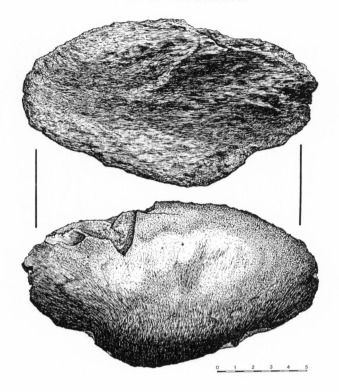

4.4 Bone flake, probably mammoth bone, University of Alaska Museum.

incorporated into the sediments of the river.

Two of my colleagues, Robert Thorson and Dale Guthrie (1984), simulated the effects of river ice on bones trapped in rivers. They froze numerous bones in large blocks of ice and dragged the blocks behind a truck, simulating the speed and types of sediment over which a river flows during breakup. The ice blocks were allowed to impact stationary objects with the same force as that created by rivers. They found that some of the bones had been abraded, faceted, striated, fractured, and flaked, becoming virtually identical to specimens from the Old Crow area that were suspected to have been modified by humans.

The power and force of a major northern river during spring breakup is an awe-inspiring sight frequently accompanied by the

Chapter 4

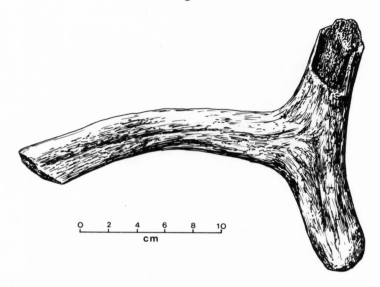

4.5 Caribou antler billet, Old Crow area, Yukon Territory (redrawn from Morlan 1980:125).

roaring and thundering of enormous blocks of colliding river ice. Because it occurs annually, this natural phenomena occurred tens of thousands of times during the Pleistocene and has probably involved millions of animal bones. A process of this duration and magnitude is easily capable of fracturing the bones of caribou. Even massive rock boulders have been flaked and faceted by this powerful force. Hundreds of thousands of the largest and most massive mammoth bones, as well as the remains of other extinct animals, have probably been flaked and fractured in this manner. By carefully sorting through the tens of thousands of bones that have been found along the river's edge, it is not surprising that some exhibit attributes similar to those produced by humans.

As a result of the vast array of taphonomic studies published during the 1970s and 1990s, it is more reasonable to postulate that the spirally fractured and flaked Pleistocene bones from the Old Crow area did not result from human activity. They are more plausibly explained by noncultural taphonomic processes, including carnivore breakage, rodent gnawing, trampling, and modification by river ice. The seemingly infinite array of noncultural phenomena that can cause bone and other materials to exhibit characteristics similar and even identical to human workmanship may never be fully defined, these noncultural attributes alone do not provide adequate evidence of human activity. As advances in taphonomic studies eliminated ever-increasing categories of bone, antler, and ivory "artifacts" from the Old Crow assemblage, the age of the accepted tools became increasingly critical to the heated debate.

Although the source of modified Pleistocene bone from the Old Crow area may best be understood as the result of noncultural processes, there still exists the group of specimens that archeologists agree are artifacts. Because of the difficulty in dating these specimens, a stalemate ensued. One group of researchers guardedly accepted these finds as evidence of Pleistocene human occupation of the Americas, and an opposing group did not because of suspicions about the quality of the C^{14} dates. This impasse lasted for more than a decade.

Finally, the advent of new technology in physics made it possible to radiocarbon date extremely small organic samples. This was essential to resolve the problem because it permitted dating the bone and antler from which the artifacts were made without destroying the specimens. In fact, the technique, known as accelerator mass spectrometry (AMS), required so little organic material that it was possible to obtain another radiocarbon date from a very small sample of the bone collagen derived from the remaining portion of the famous Old Crow flesher.

Four of the artifacts believed to be of Pleistocene age were dated (Nelson et al. 1986): the flesher, two wedges made from caribou antler, and a caribou antler billet—a hammer-like object used for flaking stone (figure 4.5). The resultant dates demonstrated that the billet was approximately 2,900 years old, the wedges were approximately 1,700 and 1,800 years old respectively, and the caribou tibia flesher previously dated to circa 27,000 years ago was in reality only about 1,350 years old. As it turned out, the flesher was almost 26,000 years younger than originally dated.

The first radiocarbon date obtained from the flesher had used a technique that dated the apatite portion of the bone, which has subsequently been demonstrated (Hassan and Ortner 1977, Hassan and Hare 1978) to be susceptible to contamination by groundwater carbonates. The elegance of the AMS technique derives from the fact that because only very small samples are required, specific components of the bone that are not subject to this type of contamination can be separated and reliably dated. The AMS dating technique is thus more accurate and reliable because it enables greater precision selecting the portions to be used in dating bone.

The work of researchers such as Dick Morlan and Bill Irving and their colleagues inspired others to embark on various new approaches to multifaceted, complex problems. The bold postulates put forth suggesting human occupation of North America more than 20,000 years ago provided the challenge necessary to stimulate further research into a vast array of natural phenomena. This has led not only to a clearer understanding of the paleoecology of eastern Beringia during the Pleistocene but also to a new phase in the quest for the origins of the first Americans.

CHAPTER 5
THE AMERICAN PALEOARCTIC TRADITION

 Occasionally it is more important to understand what is not said in scientific literature than to understand what is said. Such was the occasion of the discovery of the first evidence supporting the hypothesis that humans may have come to eastern Beringia via Asia. In 1935 Nels Nelson (1935, 1937), a curator at the American Museum of Natural History in New York, reported the discovery of unique stone tools found on an overlook near Fairbanks, Alaska. The site, which is on the University of Alaska campus, has become known as the Campus site. Nelson had worked in Europe and had traveled to Mongolia, where he had seen similar artifacts. Furthermore, Nelson (1933) had participated in the symposium in which W. A. Johnson introduced the concept that sea level fluctuations had exposed the land bridge between the two continents during the Pleistocene.

Nelson recognized the similarity between the artifacts from the Campus site and those from the Old World. He accurately described the specimens and certainly noted their technological relationship to similar artifacts found in the Old World. However, he carefully avoided any reference to the possibility that humans bearing this technological tradition may have crossed into the Americas via the Bering Land Bridge during the Pleistocene. Why should such a seemingly obvious hypothesis not appear in his writings?

During the mid 1800s many significant discoveries in Europe documented the association of humans and the extinct animals of the Pleistocene. The emerging discipline of geology demonstrated persuasively that these finds were silent testimony to the great antiquity of humans in the Old World. As news of these discoveries spread to North America it became plausible to many Americans that similar finds might exist in the New World.

Unfortunately, during this formative stage in North American archeology, the rigorous concepts and techniques employed in Europe were not implemented in the Americas. As a result, many reports of artifacts associated with Pleistocene fauna were not documented by qualified scientists at the time of their discovery. Frequently they were removed from their original context before they could be carefully examined and evaluated. The problem was further compounded by asserting great age by comparing stone tools found in the Americas with Pleistocene artifacts found in Europe.

The practice of asserting claims of great antiquity with little documentation formed a very flimsy basis for proving the great antiquity of the human species in the Americas. Inevitably there was a reaction to these excessive claims. Two geologists who have made important contributions to archeology, J. A. Gifford and G. Rapp (1985:412), have observed that by the 1880s this debate had become embroiled in a "complex interplay of discoveries, personalities, national and state politics, and sociological trends in American science which together polarized . . . opinions."

Geologists embarked on an intellectual process that archeologists and paleoecologists repeated one hundred years later. In their study of taphonomic processes in the late nineteenth century, geologists used careful field observation to identify noncultural mechanisms that modified stone to make them appear to have been modified by humans. The contexts in which these lithic pseudomorphs were found suggested great antiquity, which made the pioneering geologists question their validity as artifacts. In 1891 N. S. Shaler investigated glacial deposits. He found many flint pebbles that appeared to have been flaked by humans. He wrote of his observation (Shaler 1893:184 cited in Gifford and Rapp 1985:413):

> It became evident to me that if one searched these deposits of washed drift with the eye prepared to find implements, an unconscious choice was made of those having forms which would place them in this category; if, on the other hand, every chipped stone was taken the variety thus gathered was so great that it soon became at once both embarrassing and instructive. . . . It is clear that there are perfectly natural processes by which pebbles may be chipped in such a manner that now and then one of them may have a very artificial aspect. . . It is clear that just here we have a pitfall most dangerous for the unwary.

The American Paleoarctic Tradition

C. E. Holmes was a geologist appointed in 1910 to head the Smithsonian Institution's Bureau of American Ethnology (BAE). He published numerous, well-reasoned reviews that destroyed every claim allegedly documenting Pleistocene archeological evidence in North America (Gifford and Rapp 1985:413). Holmes's protégé at the BAE was Ales Hrdlička, a physical anthropologist. Based on his analysis of the available human skeletal material, Hrdlička concluded that humans had arrived in the New World during the Holocene. Hrdlička was vituperative in his attacks on colleagues. By the 1920s it had become unpopular, if not professionally dangerous, to suggest Pleistocene antiquity for humans in the Americas.

In this highly charged environment, it is not surprising that in 1935 Nels Nelson presented the data but left the hypothesis unstated and the conclusions to be drawn later by others. Since Nelson could not ascertain the age of either the Asian or the North American artifacts, he did not suggest that they might date to the Pleistocene. In fact, he, like Hrdlička, was a proponent of the late arrival of humans in the Americas.

As with most academic debates, it is the validity of the data that ultimately decides the issue. While the pendulum of professional consensus swings from one extreme to another, the evidence is accumulated meticulously.

The pendulum began to swing the other way as a series of discoveries were made in the American West. First was the famous Folsom type site, where extinct fauna were associated with fluted projectile points. Over time additional sites began to emerge. These sites were excavated by credible experts and were well documented while the artifacts were *in situ*. As these startling discoveries were being made, developments were taking place in eastern Beringia as well.

Froelich Rainey was the University of Alaska's first professor of anthropology and coauthored with Otto Geist a book that described the massive excavations undertaken by Geist on St. Lawrence Island in the Bering Sea. While Geist was a self-educated collector, Rainey was an academically trained archeologist. Rainey applied his knowledge of artifact classification to Geist's enormous collection

Chapter 5

5.1 Two bone points reported by Rainey from the muck deposits in the Fairbanks area. Both sides of each specimen are illustrated.

of specimens from St. Lawrence Island, and he began to amass the archeological evidence from interior areas of eastern Beringia as well.

Many of the archeological sites Rainey reported were comparatively recent and could be linked to Athapaskan-speaking peoples living in interior Alaska through the direct historic approach. However, Rainey (1939) not only recognized the uniqueness of the Campus site artifacts but also compared them with other similar specimens he had found. Furthermore, he reported a number of artifacts that had been derived from the muck deposits, which could have been associated with Pleistocene faunal remains. Though he could not ascertain the age of the deposits from which the unique Campus site or muck deposit artifacts had come, he suggested that they could be extremely old.

Rainey later teamed up with an energetic Danish archeologist, Helge Larsen. Together they discovered and excavated the famous Ipiutak site near the village of Point Hope on the coast of the Chukchi Sea. Here they found spectacular human burials. Skeletons had ivory rods inserted in their spinal columns and carved ivory eyes inset in their skulls. The burials also included elaborately carved ivory chains and large ivory pretzel-like objects. These discoveries were not only fascinating, but they also demonstrated the rich diversity and spiritual complexity in the Inuit (once known as Eskimo) culture that existed some 1,500 years ago.

During the winter of 1941–1942, Rainey and Larsen received word that Inuit hunters had found artifacts in some caves on Alaska's Seward Peninsula. In 1949 Larsen was urged to begin excavations there as a result of work undertaken at the caves by a United States Geological Survey party led by David M. Hopkins during the previous summer. Larsen led a group of students to the caves, called Trail Creek Caves after a small nearby stream, and began excavations. In the cave deposits they discovered the well-preserved bones of Pleistocene animals, including caribou, horse, bison, elk, and sheep. In the lowest stratigraphic level of a cave he designated Cave 2, he discovered the fragment of a chipped stone projectile point, which he suggested was the oldest artifact from the cave (Larsen 1968a:59–63).

The major problem confronting all of these pioneering researchers—Nelson, Geist, Rainey, and Larsen—was that they could not determine the age of the specimens they were discovering. In the absence of radiocarbon-dating, which was not developed until the late 1940s, the formidable task of dating archeological sites in Alaska was undertaken enthusiastically by Dr. Rainey's energetic young student, J. Louis Giddings. Giddings knew that the age of a tree could be determined by counting its annual growth rings. Each year during the life of a tree, it adds another layer of wood to its outer surface. Because some years are more favorable for the growth of a tree than others, the thickness of these layers vary. Trees from the same region experience the same climatic effects, so they will all grow larger rings during favorable years and thinner rings during unfavorable years. The patterns formed by this difference in tree-ring growth can be correlated between living and dead trees. The number of years that elapsed after a tree died can then be calculated. As progressively older wood is overlapped with the younger specimens, the unique patterns of tree-ring growth can be extended for

Chapter 5

thousands of years into the prehistoric past. This dating technique is called dendrochronology, and Giddings decided to apply it to his attempt to determine the age of the muck deposits.

Although the muck contained stumps from which Giddings was able to obtain samples, he was not able to link the record of growth with living trees. The result was a floating chronology which permitted him to determine the length of time a particular section of the muck had taken to accumulate, but neither a beginning nor an ending date could be established.

Giddings joined Rainey and Larsen as a field assistant in their expedition to Point Hope. He shared in their subsequent discovery of the fabulous Ipiutak site and soon became enamored with archeology. After getting his Ph.D at the University of Pennsylvania and joining the faculty at Brown University, Giddings gained recognition as the premier Alaskan archeologist. His career was

5.2 The probable techniques of manufacture of an antler projectile point of the American Paleoarctic Tradition. A length of antler (a, b) is removed, then it is deeply grooved with a burin (c) mounted in a handle for easy use until a splinter can be removed. The antler segment is rounded and worked to shape the projectile point (d).

meteoric and his accomplishments staggering. Each discovery was followed by a thorough scientific report.

Employing his knowledge of dendrochronology, Giddings embarked on an archeological survey and excavations along the Kobuk River. As a result of this work he was the first to date and chronologically order the archeological remains of the past 1,000 years of Inuit culture in the western North American arctic. However, he was troubled by an artifact he had discovered from a relatively recent archeological site that was similar to the artifacts Nelson had recognized in Mongolia and to the artifacts from the Campus site. He suspected that it had been dug from deeper within the archeological site by prehistoric peoples when constructing the house he had subsequently excavated. Years later he returned to further investigate the site, called Onion Portage, and discovered a spectacular series of stratigraphically discrete periods of human occupation extending back approximately 10,000 years. Before reaching the oldest levels containing the Campus-like artifacts at Onion Portage, Giddings unexpectedly and tragically died as a result of an automobile accident.

The work at Onion Portage was continued at Brown University and led by Giddings' student, Douglas Anderson. As the oldest archeological material at the site was discovered and described, Giddings' original hunch about the older artifacts proved cor-

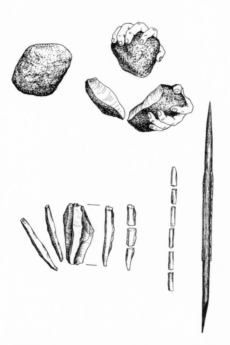

5.3 *Grooves are made in one or both sides of the antler point, and razor-sharp stone microblades, or microblade segments, are inset in the grooves to form a cutting edge.*

Chapter 5

5.4 This winter photograph of the frozen Tanana River in interior Alaska illustrates the extreme difficulty in obtaining stone to manufacture artifacts, because the ground is frozen and buried beneath snow approximately seven months of the year. The technology of the American Paleoarctic tradition largely solved this problem for prehistoric hunters.

rect. The oldest material at the site was strikingly similar to artifacts from Asia and the Campus site. Doug Anderson, an exceptional archeologist with varied interests, carried on the tradition of scholarship begun by Giddings. After describing the artifacts, Doug Anderson called them (and similar specimens from other sites) the American Paleoarctic tradition (Anderson 1970).

The American Paleoarctic tradition is a tribute to the skill and ingenuity of the prehistoric peoples of the arctic. In the Americas, these artifacts are beyond compare as a masterpiece of prehistoric stoneworking technology. They stand as silent testimony to the awe-inspiring ability of humans to cope with life in the high northern latitudes. The hallmark of this tradition is what archeologists call microblades. These are long, very thin, parallel-sided flakes of stone that have been struck from a carefully prepared stone core. Arranged end to end in a row, the microblades were set in a grooved piece of bone, wood, or antler to form a projectile point or other

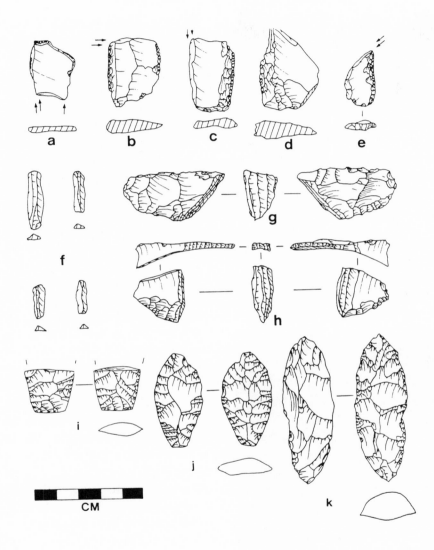

5.5 *American Paleoarctic tradition artifacts from Component II of the Dry Creek site: (a-e) burins; (f) microblades; (g-h) microblade cores; (i-k) bifaces (courtesy of Roger Powers and Ted Goebel).*

implement requiring a cutting edge made of razor-sharp stone.

The technique of manufacturing a series of thin, parallel-sided microblades from a single piece of stone is an efficient way to produce high-quality cutting edges. The alternative method for producing a cutting implement of stone is to remove irregular flakes from a block of stone until it is shaped into the desired implement, such as a projectile point or knife. By manufacturing tools in this manner, one pound of rock is required to produce approximately 20 centimeters of cutting edge. However, by using the same one pound of rock to produce microblades, as much as 1,300 centimeters of cutting edge can be produced (Hester and Grady 1982:169). In the arctic it is virtually impossible to obtain new sources of stone for about eight months of the year because the land is frozen and blanketed by snow during the winter months. By using the stone to produce microblades, these early arctic people were able to carry a small and comparatively lightweight supply of microblade cores with them and be assured that new hunting weapons could be manufactured and old weapon repaired throughout the long and difficult winter.

Since the time my former teacher, Doug Anderson (1970:64), had defined the American Paleoarctic tradition based on his analysis and comparison of the Akmak and Band 8 assemblages from the Onion Portage site, other researchers, including Don Dumond (1977), Fredrick Hadleigh West (1981), and I

5.6 Roger Powers, center foreground, wearing a white cap, and students excavating at Panguingue Creek.

The American Paleoarctic Tradition

(Dixon 1985), have expanded the definition to encompass a number of regional variants of that tradition. These regional variants are collections of artifacts similar to the artifacts from Onion Portage but exhibiting some minor differences. Diagnostic artifact types (figure 5.5) ascribed to the American Paleoarctic tradition include wedge-shaped microblade cores; larger blade cores; blades; microblades; core tablets; elongate bifaces; concave-, convex-, and straight-based projectile points or knives; burins struck on flakes and blades; burin spalls; scrapers; spokeshaves; and abraders. American Paleoarctic tradition sites have been documented over a vast area extending from the arctic coastal plain of northern Alaska as far south as the state of Washington in the Pacific Northwest.

Over a 20-year period, a variety of sites were discovered and dated, and from this meticulous and painstaking effort a framework of the age and distribution of the American Paleoarctic tradition emerged. The earliest dated sites ascribed to the American Paleoarctic tradition include Component II at the Dry Creek site (Powers and Hoffecker 1990); Locality 1 at the Gallagher Flint Station (Dixon 1975); the lower levels at the Healy Lake Village site (Cook 1969); and probably some sites ascribed to the Denali complex (West 1973, 1975, 1981) and Blue Fish Caves (Cinq-Mars 1979, Morlan and Cinq-Mars 1982). The earliest radiocarbon dates for the tradition are $10,690 \pm 250$ B.P. from Component II at Dry Creek (Powers and Hoffecker 1990:272) and $10,540 \pm 150$ B.P. from Locality 1 at the Gallagher Flint Station on Alaska's North Slope (Dixon 1975). Ironically, the Akmak assemblage at Onion Portage, the type site for the tradition, remains poorly dated but is clearly older than 8,500 B.P. (Hamilton 1970:78) and possibly is 9,500 B.P. (Anderson 1970:70). The radiocarbon chronology from all these sites suggests that the American Paleoarctic tradition was probably widespread throughout much of eastern Beringia beginning circa 10,500 B.P.

The continued persistence of the Paleoarctic tradition is demonstrated at several sites. Band 8 at the Onion Portage site is firmly dated at circa 8,000 B.P. (Anderson 1968, 1988:55), and Helge Larsen (1968a) reported bevel-based antler projectile points and microblades from Cave 9 of the Trail Creek Caves. From this site it is clear that the microblades were used as razor-sharp insets fitted into the slots of antler projectile points. These artifacts were stratigraphically above a single bifacial chalcedony projectile point. On the basis of a radiocarbon determination of 9,070 B.P. and typological comparison to Band 8 at Onion Portage, Larsen (1968a:71–72) estimated the age of these artifacts to be between 8,000 and 10,000 years old. In noncoastal areas the tradition appears to continue at Panguingue Creek where Component II has been securely dated to circa 8,600 and 7,000 B.P. (Powers and Hoffecker 1990:276,Powers and Maxwell 1986) and at Bear Cave on the Porcupine River where it is dated to circa 8,500 B.P. (Dixon et al. 1985).

During the 1970s and 1980s the geographic distribution of Paleoarctic sites became more clearly defined, and Dick Jordan (1992) suggests that sites that may be ascribed to this tradition have been reported from the Alaska Peninsula along the coast of the Gulf of Alaska and along the northwest coast of North America. Possibly the best known site is the Anangula Blade site located on Anangula Island, an islet of Umnak Island in the eastern part of the Aleutian Island chain. Bill Laughlin (1967) described the Anangula assemblage as consisting of burins, pointed tools on blades and ridge flakes, stone vessels, rubbing stones, red ochre, abraders, and house or tent depressions. Fragments of whale bone associated with hearths and the geographic location of the site indicate an economy adapted to marine mammal hunting during this period. Based on a suite of 45 radiocarbon dates (Aigner 1976, S. Laughlin et al. 1975, W. Laughlin 1975), occupation at the site began by 8,500 B.P., possibly as early as 9,000 B.P.

Eastward on the Alaska Peninsula, Paleoarctic tradition occupations are documented from the lowest levels of the Ugashik Narrows site and at Kvichak Bay. Don Dumond (1977), who named these assemblages the Ugashik Narrows phase and the Koggiung complex respectively, considers both assemblages part of the American Paleoarctic tradition. Five radiocarbon determinations indicate that these assemblages range between circa 9,000 B.P. and 7,500 B.P. (Dumond 1977, Dumond et al. 1976, Henn 1978). The Ugashik Narrows site is located along a river with a major salmon run, where large mammals such as caribou and moose may easily cross the river, which suggests that fishing and large-mammal hunting may have been important economic activities at the site.

The American Paleoarctic Tradition

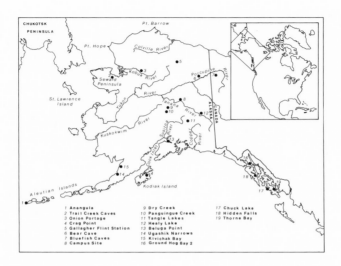

1 Anangula	9 Dry Creek	17 Chuck Lake
2 Trail Creek Caves	10 Panguingue Creek	18 Hidden Falls
3 Onion Portage	11 Tangle Lakes	19 Thorne Bay
4 Crag Point	12 Healy Lake	
5 Gallagher Flint Station	13 Beluga Point	
6 Bear Cave	14 Ugashik Narrows	
7 Bluefish Caves	15 Kivichak Bay	
8 Campus Site	16 Ground Hog Bay 2	

5.7 The location of archeological sites and locales mentioned in the text.

Doug Reger (1981) reported a small assemblage of Paleoarctic artifacts from the lowest levels of the Beluga Point site in upper Cook Inlet that date to the early Holocene. Immediately south of Cook Inlet in the Kodiak archipelago, Jordan (1992) found a Paleoarctic assemblage in the lowest cultural level at the Craig Point site that is radiocarbon-dated at 7,790 ± 620 B.P. As of 1990, this is the oldest culturally associated radiocarbon date for Kodiak Island and provides a minimum limiting date for human occupation of the island. It is also the earliest limiting date in the region for oceangoing watercraft because Kodiak Island was not connected to the mainland during the Pleistocene.

At Ground Hog Bay, located along Icy Strait not far from the city of Juneau, Alaska, Bob Ackerman, a professor at Washington State University, has excavated a site situated on a 13- to 15-meter marine terrace. The oldest cultural component is dated to approximately 9,500 B.P. based on three radiocarbon determinations (Ackerman 1968, Ackerman et al. 1979). Only eight artifacts were recovered from these lower levels, including two biface fragments. No microblades are apparently associated with this assemblage, which has led Jordan (1992) to suggest that nonmicroblade assemblages may predate subsequent microblade industries. Stratigraphically above this early material is a microblade industry dating between circa 9,000 B.P. and 4,000 B.P. The coastal orientation of this site indicates economic activities focused on the harvesting of adjacent marine resources.

U.S. Forest Service archeologists (Davis 1989) describe an early microblade industry from the Hidden Falls site on Baranof Island. Based on a suite of 13 radiocarbon dates and stratigraphic interpretation, Davis (1989:159–198) suggests the microblade industry dates to circa 9,000 B.P.

Farther to the south on Prince of Wales Island, Chuck Holmes (Holmes et al. 1989) has reported the Thorne Bay site, which also may be attributed to the American Paleoarctic tradition. The cultural occupation at the Thorne Bay site was approximately 7,500 B.P., based on three radiocarbon determinations.

The Chuck Lake site (Ackerman et al. 1985, Okada et al. 1989) is situated on Heceta Island off the northwestern shore of Prince of Wales Island in southeastern Alaska. A crew of Japanese archeologists under the direction of the husband-and-wife team of professors Hiroaki and Atsuko Okada have been investigating the site along with Ackerman. A microblade industry is reported from Locality 1 that the investigators believe dates to circa 8,000 B.P., based on interpretation of several radiocarbon determinations from this locality. Faunal material associated with this occupation includes marine mammal, fish, land mammal, and bird remains.

The documentation and accurate dating of this series of Paleoarctic sites along the northeastern Pacific rim during the 1970s and 1980s led Jordan (1992) to suggest classifying these sites as Maritime Paleoarctic tradition, based on their obvious marine economic orientation and the fact that they exhibit the major typological traits defining the Paleoarctic tradition. These sites range in age between circa 9,000 B.P. and 7,500 B.P. and are distributed from the Aleutian Islands along the Gulf of Alaska southward along the northwest coast of North America until they reach their southern limit in the state of Washington, where they are dated to circa 6,500 B.P. (Dumond 1980:990). Based on the meticulous accumu-

The American Paleoarctic Tradition

lation of data by many dedicated researchers, it slowly has been revealed that the American Paleoarctic tradition first appeared in the northern regions of eastern Beringia by about 10,600 B.P. and subsequently spread southward along the coasts of Alaska and British Columbia prior to 9,000 B.P. The later distribution along the northwest coast of North America suggests that by this time these peoples were skillful and experienced in marine mammal hunting and fishing.

The success of this technology in adapting to the rigors of the North American arctic is clearly indicated by the vast number of archeological sites containing microblades that have been found from Alaska to Greenland and as far south as the state of Washington. The importance of this technological approach to arctic survival also is documented by the great length of time that this method of tool manufacture persisted, which may be as late as 1,500 years ago in some areas (Dixon 1985). Though the earliest evidence of this tradition is called the American Paleoarctic tradition, later aspects of it are called the Arctic Small Tool tradition in coastal areas where it appears to have the most continuous record and the Late Denali complex in the Alaskan interior. Because many of the technological traits that characterized the American Paleoarctic tradition can be traced over a long period of time to prehistoric Inuit material culture (Larsen 1968b), some archeologists believe that the bearers of the American Paleoarctic tradition may have been the remote ancestors of the Inuit and Aleut.

The gifted Scandinavian archeologist Helge Larsen (1968b) suggested that a continuum in Inuit technology can be recognized in the transition from the American Paleoarctic tradition use of microblades as projectile point insets to the subsequent manufacture and use of bifacially flaked and ground side blades. The burin reflects concurrent development from flaking to grinding through time and is considered essential for the manufacture of antler, ivory, and bone projectile points and inset slots. By carefully tracing the development of specific technological traits, Larsen came to regard the Arctic Small Tool tradition that flourished in Alaska between circa 4,200 and 1,200 B.P. (Anderson 1968) as a later phase of the American Paleoarctic tradition.

Chapter 5

Larsen (1968b:339) provided what may be the most useful, geographically encompassing definition of these associated material cultural traits in stating,

> We must consider the American microblades in question as the northeastern branch of a Circumpolar Microblade tradition, or, to be specific, of a Circumpolar Side Blade tradition. By using the later version, we may include the latter forms of side blades, which range from blades, as we know them from Siberia as well as from North America.

Larsen went on to state,

> The fact that the side blade tradition as well as the core and blade technique and burins or grooving-tools obviously derived from burins occur in the Inuit culture seems to indicate that people with some relationship to the Eskimo were involved. Although I believe that this complex constitutes the roots of Eskimo culture, I do not equate it with the Eskimo culture.

In other words, he viewed them at different ends of a long technological continuum beginning with the American Paleoarctic tradition and continuing through time to contemporary Inuit, or Eskimo, culture.

It was clear to pioneering arctic prehistorians such as Larsen that artifacts of the American Paleoarctic tradition bear great similarity to artifacts of what is called the Upper Paleolithic, or the later part of the Old Stone Age, in the Old World. It was this great similarity that caught the attention of Geist, Nelson, Giddings, and Rainey and still fascinates archeologists today. Because of this great similarity, many prehistorians believed that the specimens from eastern Beringia should be of comparable age to similar artifacts from the Old World, where they were firmly dated to the late Pleistocene and had been recovered in association with extinct ice age fauna. Some speculated that perhaps the early mammoth hunters in America were somehow derived from this early Paleolithic technology. Not until the 1970s and 1980s were the age of both the earlier and later manifestations of the American Paleoarctic tradition defined. As a result of this work, it became apparent that

The American Paleoarctic Tradition

the American Paleoarctic tradition was actually younger than the Llano complex. For the Llano complex to reach the American Southwest by circa 11,500 B.P., there had to be a tradition in eastern Beringia even older than the American Paleoarctic tradition if humans had first entered the Americas via eastern Beringia.

* * * * * * *

Gary Selinger and I had parted in New York City. He was to return to Alaska with one-half of each sample we had collected. I was carrying the remaining tissue samples and the fluted projectile points from the Smithsonian directly to Tom Loy. We had already sent Loy a tissue sample from Blue Babe and the fluted points housed at the University of Alaska Museum. The remaining fluted projectile points from the National Museum in Canada were to be sent directly from Ottawa. We would soon have everything we needed to apply his new technique to the artifacts and hopefully to determine whether or not they had been used to hunt extinct Pleistocene animals. My excitement mounted as I neared what I hoped might be at least a partial resolution to this long-standing problem.

As the aircraft began to descend in Vancouver, the stewardess distributed the usual customs cards asking what you were bringing into Canada. I swiftly filled out the questionnaire until I came to the part asking whether I was bringing any animal products into the country. How was I going to explain that I was importing the flesh of extinct animals into Canada? What if they wouldn't let me bring the samples into the country? Suppose they confiscated the mammoth meat? Panic began to set in when I realized that I had little time after landing in Vancouver to catch my connecting flight to Victoria. I began to toy with the idea of not mentioning my stash of ancient flesh. However, reason soon prevailed, and I filled out the form honestly and prepared to explain my curious cargo if necessary.

After deplaning I was directed to customs and the agricultural inspection, where I was questioned by a polite young woman. She asked what type of animal products I was carrying. She became

Chapter 5

intrigued when I told her that they were tissue samples from extinct Pleistocene animals and quite naturally asked why I was bringing them to Canada. As I began to explain our research, she became increasingly interested and wanted to learn more and more. She was fascinated by the problem and the research approach. Each question I answered led her to ask another question until I realized that I would surely miss my flight to Victoria. When I pointed out my need for haste she cheerfully let me pass.

I managed to catch the last flight to Victoria that night. Although I was exhausted, I had difficulty sleeping in anticipation of what we might begin to learn the following day. We were closer than anyone had ever been to solving this 50-year-old problem. But would all this effort and complex reasoning yield fruitful results? I would begin to find out the next day.

CHAPTER 6
MINCING MAMMOTH MEAT

 The fresh scent of the ocean was in the air as I walked through the streets of Victoria to meet Tom Loy. I arrived early and waited in the foyer of the Curatorial Towers where most of the offices of the British Columbia Provincial Museum are located. When Loy arrived we walked to his laboratory, which was several blocks away. I began to brief him on the results of my visit to the Smithsonian Institution and the American Museum of Natural History. As we discussed our research plans, I was impressed with the breadth of his imagination for applications of his new techniques. I also was disappointed to learn that the fluted projectile points from the National Museum of Man in Ottawa had not arrived. It was my hope to work with as many of the fluted points as possible, and those housed in Ottawa constituted a large proportion of the specimens.

Loy's laboratory was located in the geriatric unit of Victoria General Hospital. Elderly men smoking cigarettes sat in wheelchairs outside the front door. I wondered what they would say if they knew the small box in my hand contained the flesh of animals that had died more than 20,000 years ago. We went up the elevator and entered a laboratory cluttered with bottles, beakers, assorted glassware, and tubing. It would take days to prepare samples for analysis, and we began the meticulous process immediately. Because the methods were designed to identify very small amounts of residue, we had to be extremely careful to keep everything clean and not risk mixing even the smallest amounts of tissue of one species with another.

We duplicated the notes I had taken for each sample of prehistoric tissue collected at the American Museum so that Loy would have an accurate record for each specimen. Our research strategy was to use blood from clearly identified extant and extinct species for comparison with the residues preserved on the fluted projectile points.

Chapter 6

As we began to work Loy explained the process. Six independent tests would be used to identify and analyze the residues observed on the artifacts. Initially, the artifacts would be tested for the presence of hemoglobin using two different and independent tests. Third, a microscope would be used to examine surfaces for residue concentrations and microfossils, such as tiny bits of hair. The magnifications would range between 100 and 1000 times the size of the objects we were observing. However, lower magnifications would be used to surficially examine the projectile points themselves for residue. Fourth, we would use isoelectric focusing (IEF) to separate the proteins in the extracted residues from four of the projectile points that had sufficient residue to permit this test. IEF separations sort molecules into distinct groups by their native pH, or acid base, in a specially prepared, complex buffered gel. IEF had been used to identify the origin of various meat samples as a test of meat purity (Sinclair and Slattery 1982) and the results demonstrated that small differences in the isoelectric point (pI) between species in a number of molecules enabled a clear differentiation between even closely related species such as sheep and goats. Fifth, we would use hemoglobin crystallization techniques that Loy had employed in his original work to identify species of origin. Under certain conditions each species' hemoglobin forms a crystalline shape unique to that species and different from all other species. By comparing the hemoglobin crystals grown from the residues with the crystals for known species, the species represented on the projectile points could be identified. Sixth, he would identify and measure red blood cells whenever possible. Because red blood cell size varies from species to species, this theoretically could provide another independent source of data to test against the results of the other techniques. It was exciting to think that these methods held the potential to expand the analytical frontiers of archeological science. Knowing little chemistry or microbiology, I placed myself totally in Loy's hands.

Our first job was to make a liquor from the fossil tissue samples I had brought from the American Museum. We tackled the mammoth first. We extracted a small amount of tissue from the sealed vial that I had labeled in New York a few days earlier. Using a very

Mincing Mammoth Meat

sharp scalpel we chopped it into many small pieces. The minced mammoth meat was rehydrated by adding deionized water and a minute amount of fungicide to prevent the possible growth of fungi. The vial was sealed to prevent contamination. As we began agitating this concoction using a mechanical rocker, we were delighted to see the mixture turn a reddish-brown color within a matter of minutes. This suggested that the sample was rich in blood.

This liquid was to become our standard, which would be used for comparison in analyzing the residues extracted from the projectile points. If the blood residues from the projectile points had the same shape of hemoglobin crystals and the same size of red blood cells as those from the tissue we knew to be mammoth, then we could be reasonably certain that the blood on the points was also mammoth. Similarly, we would compare the blood residue on the points with the blood samples we had collected from living bison, extinct bison, Dall sheep, and other mammals. It would take at least 48 hours before we were satisfied that the parent liquid was suitable for experimental purposes and would react positively to at least two independent tests to determine the presence of hemoglobin.

The excitement began to wear off as the tedious routine of laboratory bench work became grinding monotony. We repeated the above process for each of the species. Each projectile point we subjected to rigorous examination and recording, drawing each projectile point on a special form and recording its catalog number along with a summary of a host of other information regarding where it was found and its curatorial history. We examined each point first under a microscope to identify the presence or absence of residues. If we observed residues on the surface, we mapped their distribution on the artifact on the drawing we had made of the projectile point. We made notes on these forms to record our observations and research results.

At this level of analysis the artifact became analogous to an archeological site with mapping of surface features and recording of depositional layers of residue. The minute objects preserved on the points' surfaces became like artifacts within the larger site. Collectively they could tell at least some of the history of the projectile point. As we continued the meticulous process of drawing and recording the information associated with each projectile point, I reflected on the very different histories associated with each point. They were derived from archeological discoveries spanning more than forty years. It was ironic to contemplate that different projectile points could have been made by the same man thousands of years ago, only to be discovered long after his death by different archeologists and consequently deposited in different museums thousands of miles apart.

Careful examination of the points revealed minute amounts of sediment still clinging to the surfaces of some specimens, suggesting they had come from a variety of depositional environments. Others had been subjected to stringent and destructive curatorial treatments and analytical techniques that had left their surfaces less natural. Some specimens had been vigorously scrubbed and cleaned. The little residue that remained was too small to be extracted for analysis. On other specimens we could detect no residue at all. They may never have been used by prehistoric peoples, or they may have been cleaned thoroughly by the archeologists who had studied them. Some specimens were contaminated by the ink and lacquer

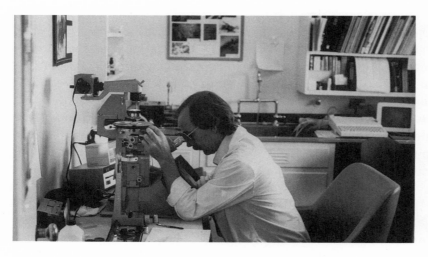

6.1 Tom Loy at work in his lab at Victoria, B.C.

used to catalog them. Others had the remains of compounds used to make molds from which replicas had been cast. All of these factors made this difficult task even more challenging.

As the days wore on, it became increasingly clear that we would not be able to finish the work in the time I had allotted. However, we would be able to accomplish some of our work and hopefully have some results before my departure. Most importantly, we would be able to grow the mammoth hemoglobin crystals, and this in itself would be an exciting and significant accomplishment. This was one of life's rare opportunities, which most of us never experience: the opportunity to view, for the first time, something no other human has ever seen.

The first laboratory examples of mammoth hemoglobin crystals were grown two days after we had mixed our control sample of mammoth tissue and water. After testing positive for hemoglobin, the hemoglobin molecules were forced to precipitate as crystals by the addition of specific salts in specific concentrations and the subsequent increase of salt concentration by evaporation of the parent liquid (Loy 1983). We excitedly watched these first crystalline aggregates grow under the microscope. We photographed and drew them (figure 6.2) and constructed a model of the crystal out of modeling clay. These models would be used for comparison with crystals grown from the residues extracted from the artifacts

Although the crystal growth was exciting, I was disturbed by my lack of knowledge of crystallography, chemistry, and microbiology. For all I knew, the crystals I was observing under the microscope could be from any of the buffers or salts mixed to force their growth or from some other source. However, Loy assured me that these other crystals could be readily recognized by their characteristic shape and that the ones we were observing were certainly mammoth hemoglobin. To make matters worse for me, the crystals would bloom and be clearly visible for only a short period of time, and then they would dissolve and disappear. During this interval they had to be observed, photographed, and sketched. There remained no permanent record of them having occurred except for the notes and photos of the investigator.

We observed red blood cells from the fossil tissue of

Chapter 6

various species that we were using as standards in three size ranges: 4.8 to 5.5 microns, 8 to 9 microns, and 9.4 to 11 microns (a micron is 1/1000 of a millimeter). Loy attributed variation in size within these groups to distortions in the red blood cell membranes during the initial deposition and drying phase of residue formation and during rehydration for analysis. Most of the red blood cells we observed were "ghost cells" (that is, the cell membrane without its hemoglobin contents), which varied from the normally smooth biconcave discs. We identified the red blood cells of the woolly mammoth from the parent liquid standard and within the fossil tissue samples through microscopy. Preserved red blood cells could be identified and measured within the tissue capillaries, the red blood cell size observed for mammoth ranging between 9.4 and 11 microns. These large red blood cells are diagnostic because of their relatively large size in comparison to other species that could possibly be represented among the analyzed residues.

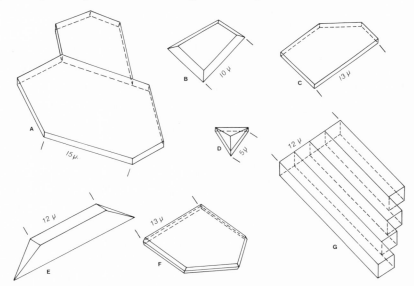

6.2 *Hemoglobin crystals grown, identifying (a) woolly mammoth* (Mammuthus primigenius); *(b) American bison* (Bison bison); *(c) Pleistocene bison* (Bison pricus); *(d) Mountain sheep* (Ovis dalli), *(e) caribou* (Rangifer tarandus), *(f) musk ox* (Ovibos moschatus), (g) brown bear (Ursus arcto) *(from laboratory drawings, Loy and Dixon 1987 and Loy and Wood 1989:454.)*

Mincing Mammoth Meat

The isoelectric focusing proved to be even more incomprehensible to me than the growing and identifying of the hemoglobin crystals. IEF required the complex preparation of a gelatin, which, when finished, looked like a sheet of rather thick, clear Jello. Drops of residue extracted from four of the projectile points were placed on the gel and forced to migrate along it by the application of an electric current. Only four of the projectile points had sufficient residue to run this as well as the other tests and still save some residue for future research. The results of isoelectric focusing were interpreted by comparison with the pI (isoelectric point) standards lane. The pI value of each of the major peaks was calculated (Nelson et al. 1986), and coefficients of similarity were calculated for comparison between the unknown sample and various reference standards from known species. However, the comparison of identical species did not yield a 100% match. Usually the blood of identical species only matches between 60% and 85%. Even totally unrelated species showed a match between 10% and 20%. On many of the projectile points, blood residues resulted from multiple usage of a specific tool in contact with two or more species. The residue from one point yielded a coefficient that Loy felt was not as ambiguous as the others, a 58% match with *Mammuthus primigenius.* All others suggested the presence of more than one species' blood. The identification of residue of two or more species was more clearly established through hemoglobin crystallization.

Slowly these independent analytical methods began to produce results. The first species we identified on the points was modern bison *(Bison bison).* Later we identified Dall sheep *(Ovis dalli).* Then it happened: we identified mammoth! I had hypothesized that we would not discover mammoth remains on these projectile points because I suspected that the points were younger in Alaska than in the lower 48 states and that by the time they were used in eastern Beringia mammoth already would have been extinct. To compound my confusion, one of the projectile points that tested positive for mammoth was not fluted but came from a well-dated archeological site I had excavated a few years earlier. I knew the site was approximately 9,500 years old; if the identification of mammoth was correct, this would be the most recent documentation of

Chapter 6

mammoth anywhere in North America! When the time we had to devote to this research was over, we had not finished the analysis of all the fluted points. I was confused and needed time to more thoroughly digest what I had learned and observed. Should I disregard the results of our analysis because I did not fully understand the methods or because the results did not confirm my hypothesis? There was a high degree of art in the laboratory procedures and an element of subjectivity in the identifications. I needed time to think. We agreed to wait until we received the rest of the fluted points to resume the study. Little did we realize that it would be almost a year before we could complete the analysis.

Although I was confused and frustrated by my experiences in Victoria, I felt that ultimately order would emerge from what at that time appeared to be confusion. It was unreasonable to expect resolution of these complex problems in just a few weeks. We were drawing upon recent techniques in biochemistry to address a long-standing archeological problem, and I lacked the experience or expertise to adequately evaluate our methods or results. I was confident, however, that blood residues were preserved on the projectile points and that they did have a story to tell. In my role as museum curator I was convinced of the need for sound curatorial procedures that would guard against contamination, destruction, or modification of specimens as they were received from the field. Museum collections would play an increasingly important role in addressing a wide array of research problems as the new technologies in biochemistry were applied to human prehistory.

CHAPTER 7

THE NENANA COMPLEX

 The saga of the search for the blood of extinct mammals on fluted projectile points nearly came to a standstill as the bureaucracy of the National Museum of Man seemed unable to respond to my request for the loan of the fluted projectile points from Canada. I called my colleagues Don Clark and Jacques Cinq-Mars, the archeologists along with Dick Morlan who had discovered and reported these points. By eliciting their help, the points were sent directly to Tom Loy in British Columbia. We scheduled a time for my trip to Victoria; however, I was able to return to Victoria for only a brief time. Although the specimens from the Canadian National Museum arrived, we once again were unable to complete the analysis within the time we had available. Then other responsibilities took precedence over my research for the next several months.

The Alaska Anthropological Association annual meetings were held in Fairbanks in 1987. I especially enjoyed the meetings because we had two stimulating house guests. One of them was Tom Dillehay, an archeologist working on a controversial site in Chile reportedly at least 13,000 years old. The other was my old friend Dick Jordan, who was making exciting and unexpected discoveries on Kodiak Island, Alaska.

Jordan and I had first met in 1970 when he was a student at Dartmouth College and I was a student at the University of Alaska. We both did fieldwork under John Cook, whose academic career made him part of a complex web of associations that touched many archeologists in Alaska. Cook had graduated from Dartmouth College, studied under Louis Giddings at Brown University, and joined the faculty at the University of Alaska while finishing his dissertation on the Healy Lake Village site for his doctorate at the University of Wisconsin.

In 1972 Jordan and I both received George C. Marshall Fellowships to study in Copenhagen at the National Museum of Denmark

Chapter 7

under Helge Larsen, the excavator of the Trail Creek Caves and the famous Ipiutak site near Point Hope, Alaska. With the housing shortage in Copenhagen, Jordan graciously invited me to stay with him and his wife. We shared an apartment there for three months while we pored over artifact collections under the gentle guidance of Helge Larsen. While Jordan went on to conduct field research in the eastern arctic with Bill Fitzhugh from the Smithsonian Institution, I continued my field research in Alaska.

Jordan and I both had worked as excavators at the Healy Lake Village site in interior Alaska along with other students who would later make contributions to archeology in the North. A lot has happened in the archeology of interior Alaska in the almost 20 years since then. Healy Lake was the first of several discoveries that would allow us to piece together a picture of the people who lived in interior Alaska about 10,500 or 11,500 years ago, prior to the American Paleoarctic tradition.

* * * * * * *

The excavations at the Healy Lake Village site were directed by John Cook, an excellent field archeologist who applied his considerable skill and perseverance toward excavating this site. The site was difficult to excavate and interpret because it lacked natural stratigraphy, which rendered true stratigraphic association between artifacts impossible. Because of the lack of recognizable stratigraphic levels, Cook excavated the site in arbitrary 2-inch levels. The word *Chindadn* meant ancestor in Athapaskan, and he (Cook 1969) named the artifacts from the lowest and oldest levels the Chindadn complex. The few artifacts recovered from the Chindadn complex are characterized by triangular and teardrop-shaped points and knives; these were associated with two microblade cores and a few microblades. The radiocarbon dates from the lowest levels suggested these artifacts were possibly 10,500 to 11,000 years old. Although the microblades and microblade cores were familiar artifacts clearly associated with the American Paleoarctic tradition, the relatively small, thin, teardrop-shaped and triangular shaped bifacial stone tools had not been recognized before this discovery.

The Nenana Complex

In 1973 Chuck Holmes, another alumnus of Healy Lake and the University of Alaska, made an important discovery. Holmes was examining exposures along the Parks Highway north of McKinley National Park. Along Dry Creek he discovered microblades eroding from a bluff. Preliminary investigations suggested he had discovered a deeply buried stratified American Paleoarctic site. Over the next decade this site, named Dry Creek, and the surrounding Nenana River valley were subjected to intensive archeological investigations, which yielded more knowledge about interior Alaskan prehistory. The leader in these studies was Roger Powers, an expert in the prehistory of Russia, whom John Cook had recruited to the faculty of the University of Alaska after they had been graduate students together at the University of Wisconsin. With the aid of his students and colleagues, Powers excavated Dry Creek and several other important sites in the Nenana River valley.

In a separate stratigraphic level below the American Paleoarctic tradition artifacts, Powers and his students discovered a different

7.1 Left to right: Dick Jordan, Dennis Stanford, and James Dixon at the Walker Road site, one of the type sites for the Nenana complex, interior Alaska (courtesy of Charles Mason).

and older assemblage of artifacts. These artifacts were named the Nenana complex, after the Nenana River valley in which they were discovered. The Nenana complex is unique because it lacks microblades and is perhaps best characterized by relatively small, thin triangular and teardrop-shaped bifaces similar to the ones recovered from the Chindadn complex discovered at the Healy Lake Village site. Retrospectively, it is reasonable to speculate that the lowest levels at the Healy Lake Village site contain a Nenana complex assemblage mixed with a few later American Paleoarctic tradition artifacts. The intermixed microblade cores and microblades probably result from the inability of arbitrary 2-inch levels to isolate precisely the stratigraphic position of artifacts at the Healy Lake Village site.

After the discovery of the Nenana complex at Dry Creek, two other sites were also discovered in the Nenana River valley, the Walker Road and Moose Creek sites. Together these three sites serve as the type sites for defining the Nenana complex. The Nenana complex is defined (Powers and Hoffecker 1990) solely on the basis of lithic artifacts because associated organic remains are rare. Diagnostic artifact types include 1) triangular and teardrop-shaped projectile points and knives, 2) straight- or concave-based lanceolate projectile points, 3) perforators, 4) end and side scrapers, 5) burins, 6) hammer and anvil stones, 7) unifacial knives and scrapers, 8) gravers, 9) abraders, and 10) blades or blade-like flakes. Retouched flakes, small stone wedges *(piece esquillée),* and lithic debitage are also associated with these sites. These diagnostic lithic traits are identified from Components I at the Dry Creek, Walker Road, and Moose Creek sites, where these artifacts occur in excellent stratigraphic context in conjunction with concurrent radiocarbon determinations (Powers and Hoffecker 1990) (figure 7.2).

Radiocarbon dates from Components I at the Walker Road and Dry Creek sites range between circa 11,800 and 11,000 B.P., averaging circa 11,300 B.P. (Powers and Hoffecker 1990:278). The age of the Nenana complex is established not only by radiocarbon dating but also by the stratigraphy in the Nenana River valley, where Nenana complex sites are repeatedly found near the bottom of thick sections of windblown sediments that began to accumulate during the early

The Nenana Complex

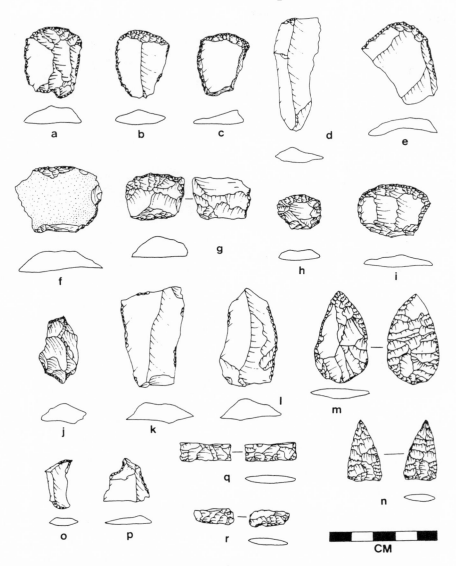

7.2 *Nenana complex artifacts from Dry Creek, Component I, and Walker Road, Component I: (a-i) end scrapers, Dry Creek; (j) stone wedge piece esquillée, Dry Creek; (k,l) blades, Dry Creek; (m) teardrop-shaped biface, Walker Road; (n) triangular projectile point, Dry Creek; (o,p) perforators; (q,r) basal fragments, triangular projectile points (courtesy of Roger Powers and Ted Goebel).*

Birch interval. Since the original discovery and excavation of the Dry Creek, Moose Creek, and Walker Road sites, several other archeological sites ascribed to the Nenana complex have been found and excavated in the Nenana (Powers and Hoffecker 1990), Teklanika (Phippen 1988), and Tanana (Lively 1988, Holmes and Yesner, personal communication 1990) river valleys in central interior Alaska.

A graduate student at the University of Alaska, Peter Phippen, excavated the Owl Ridge site. This stratified site had been occupied several times over the past several thousand

7.3 Chuck Holmes at the Broken Mammoth site. The Tanana River is in the background.

years. It is located on a south-facing tributary to the Teklanika River valley. The earliest occupation, Component I, occurs in a stratigraphic context similar to that of Nenana complex sites in the Nenana River valley. Although few artifacts were found in this level, those present are similar to the Nenana complex and there is no evidence of a microblade industry. This comparison is supported by a radiocarbon date of $11,340 \pm 150$ B.P. (Beta–11209) (Phippen 1988).

Another University of Alaska graduate student, Ralph Lively, reported similar artifacts from the Chugwater site within the Tanana River valley (Lively 1988). Based on comparison with specimens from Components I at Dry Creek, Walker Road, and Moose Creek, he (Lively 1988:78–79, 102) believes the artifacts are similar to those of the Nenana complex. The artifacts he found include end scrapers, end/side scrapers, triangular projectile points, and teardrop-shaped bifacial projectile points or knives.

Chuck Holmes, who first identified the Dry Creek site, has discovered what may prove to be the most important Nenana

The Nenana Complex

7.4 David Yesner, center foreground, during excavations at the Broken Mammoth site.

complex site yet discovered. He (Holmes 1990) named it the Broken Mammoth site because of a piece of broken mammoth bone he found on the slope in front of the site. The site is situated on a bluff overlooking the Tanana River not far from its junction with Shaw Creek. Another related site, the Mead site (Pewe et al. 1965, Holmes 1990), is located approximately one kilometer to the northeast. The Broken Mammoth site was discovered and tested by Holmes during the summer of 1989, and he and David Yesner initiated preliminary excavations in 1990. They have discovered a record of three important, stratigraphically distinct periods when humans occupied the site. The site was last occupied by peoples who manufactured and used microblades approximately 2,500 years ago. Stratigraphically below the 2,500 B.P. microblade-bearing levels, a few artifacts represent evidence of a brief occupation. The oldest occupation is preserved approximately 180–190 centimeters, or about 5 feet, below the surface. Radiocarbon dates of 10,790 ± 230 B.P. (WSU 4019) and 11,040 ± 260 B.P. (UGA 6257) (Holmes 1990, personal communication 1990) indicate the lower levels of the Broken Mammoth site are approximately the same age as other Nenana complex archeological sites. The preliminary information from the excavations at both the Broken Mammoth and Mead sites suggests the absence of microblade technology in the early levels and that they are technologically related to the Nenana complex. Their stratigraphic position near the base of late Pleistocene/early Holocene loess deposits and the preliminary radiocarbon chronology further demonstrate they belong to the Nenana complex.

Chapter 7

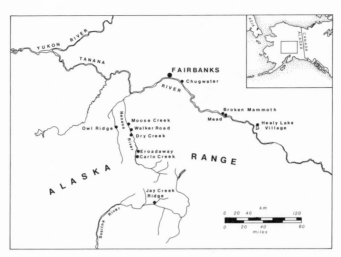

7.5 The location of sites related to the Nenana complex.

Although fragmentary and poorly preserved faunal remains were found at Dry Creek, the Broken Mammoth and Mead sites are the only known sites dating to this time period containing a wide variety of well-preserved remains documenting the animals hunted by these early peoples. Preliminary analysis of the bones by Yesner and Holmes (personal communication 1990) indicate that several species of birds including cranes, ducks, swans, and geese were consumed at the site. In addition, the bones of hare, ground squirrel, beaver, bison, caribou, and possibly elk or moose have been identified from the earliest occupations (Holmes 1990, personal communication 1990). Another important discovery is the identification of salmonoid fish scale from these same levels, suggesting that these peoples fished for salmon as well as hunted.

Tusk fragments of proboscideans, either mammoth or mastodon, have been recovered from the early occupations at both the Mead and Broken Mammoth sites. A small stone chip imbedded in a worked tusk fragment from the Broken Mammoth site and the medial segment of a broken dowel-like object made of proboscidean ivory from the Mead site suggest that mammoth or mastodon either

7.6 Artifacts from the Jay Creek Ridge site: (a-d) retouched flakes; (e) biface fragment, (f) scraper; (g) biface fragment; (h-k) probable projectile point tips; (l-p) projectile point and/or knife fragments.

Chapter 7

were hunted or their ivory was scavenged from the landscape by occupants of these sites (Holmes 1990, personal communication 1990).

During Loy's and my analysis of residues preserved on the lithic artifacts from the Jay Creek Ridge site we discovered that the stone had come into contact with mammoth, bison, and sheep. If our highly experimental research was correct and there was truly mammoth blood on these specimens, this would be the youngest documentation of mammoth in the Americas and would suggest that mammoth persisted in eastern Beringia as late as 9,500 years ago.

Jay Creek Ridge is one of four other sites that have been excavated in central interior Alaska, which, although later than the Nenana complex, may be related. These are Component I at the Carlo Creek site (Bowers 1978a, 1978b, 1978c and 1980a), the Jay Creek Ridge site (Dixon 1986, unpublished notes, UAF Museum), the Eroadaway site (Holmes 1988), and Component II at the Owl Ridge site (Phippen 1988). All of these sites range in age between 9,500 B.P. and 8,500 B.P. They all bear similarity to the Nenana complex because they exhibit a bifacial technology similar to that of the Nenana complex and lack evidence of a microblade industry. The ovate and triangular bifacial forms from these sites may bear morphological similarity to examples in the Nenana complex. Although not part of the original definition of the Nenana complex as described by Powers and Hoffecker (1990), the data may suggest that these sites represent a persistence of the Nenana complex in interior Alaska until at least 8,500 B.P.

The earliest occupation at the Jay Creek Ridge site is approximately 9,500 B.P. based on six radiocarbon dates (unpublished C[14] determinations, Dixon 1986, 1987, on file, University of Alaska Museum). This occupation was discovered in an ancient soil approximately 20 centimeters below a volcanic ash that was deposited sometime between 5,100 and 5,900 B.P. (Dixon and Smith 1990:392–394). Charcoal identified from a hearth at the site documents birch (probably dwarf, based on the small diameter of the fragments) and willow, which suggests a shrub tundra environment in the site vicinity at the time of occupation. The artifacts from this

The Nenana Complex

level are characterized by concave-based projectile points manufactured of flat, thin flakes of argillite and basalt, which exhibit basal and lateral edge grinding (figure 7.6: l, m, n). There are no microblades, nor is there evidence of microblade technology from this level at this site. The assemblage also contains an end scraper and small triangular projectile points or knives. The Folsom-like projectile points are similar to examples from the American Southwest, but the ones from the Jay Creek Ridge site lack fluting. The small triangular bifaces suggest similarities with the Nenana complex. Although there are no identifiable faunal remains from this component, the site commands an approach to a mineral lick currently used by Dall sheep and other large mammals. This suggests that large mammal-hunting may have been the most important economic activity associated with this site.

Peter Bowers excavated the Carlo Creek site, which was first occupied about 8,500 B.P. (Bowers 1978a, 1978b, 1980a). Faunal remains suggest that this first occupation was a fall/winter hunting camp where caribou, sheep, and ground squirrel were processed (Bowers 1980a:136). The stone used to manufacture artifacts appears to have been heated to make it easier to flake. The artifacts recovered include percussion-flaked elongate bifaces, biface frag-

7.7 Artifacts typologically ascribed to the Nenana complex: (a-d) teardrop bifaces, Healy Lake, Levels 7 and 8; (e,f,g) scrapers, Dry Creek, Component I; (h) triangular biface (rearticulated fragments), Dry Creek, Component I; (i,) triangular projectile points, Healy Lake Villages site, Level 7; (j) triangular projectile points, Dry Creek, Component I, (k) triangular projectile point, Healy Lake Village Site, Level 7.

ments, retouched flakes, and lithic debitage (Bowers 1980a:84). No evidence of a microblade or burin industry is associated with this assemblage.

The second occupation, or Component II, at the Owl Ridge site is approximately 75 centimeters below the surface and was occupied sometime between 9,500 and 7,500 B.P. based on four radiocarbon determinations (Phippen 1988:3, 77). The artifact assemblage from Component II at the Owl Ridge site is small. Only one ovate and one subtriangular biface were recovered. The component lacks evidence of microblade and burin technology. The spatial distribution of cobbles has been interpreted as the remains of a possible tent ring (Phippen 1988:118–123), which is a ring of stones placed along the perimeter of a tent to secure it in the wind.

The Eroadaway site is another important discovery by the energetic Chuck Holmes. Its age has been determined by a single radiocarbon date of 8,640 ± 170 B.P. (WSU–3683) (Holmes 1988:3). The site contains straight- and slightly concave-based projectile points, some of which exhibit edge grinding; bifaces; unifacial flake tools; and lithic debitage (Holmes 1988, personal communication 1990). Preserved spruce needles and burned twigs also were recovered from the site, suggesting the proximity of black spruce to the site circa 8,500 B.P. (Holmes 1988:4). Significantly, this site also lacks evidence of microblade technology.

Although relatively little is known of the lifeways of the people of the Nenana complex, there is enough preliminary information to formulate some tentative interpretations. At the Dry Creek site the remains of sheep and elk document that large mammals were taken. Numerous gastroliths, or tiny stones from the gizzards of birds, suggest that birds, probably grouse and ptarmigan, were important in the diet of these early hunters. Although the identifications are still preliminary, the excellent faunal preservation at the Broken Mammoth site demonstrates a wider range of prey, including what is probably heavy seasonal exploitation of migratory waterfowl. Given the information we have, it is reasonable to assume that these northern hunters moved to different types of camps throughout the year depending on seasonal peaks in fish and local concentrations of the animals they hunted. They effectively harvested a variety of

The Nenana Complex

large and small mammals, waterfowl, and probably fish (including salmon).

All sites ascribed to the Nenana complex were small camps occupied by a few individuals. In most cases fires appear to have been built directly on the surface of the ground with little or no preparation of the area. Charcoal is generally scattered and relatively scarce for dating purposes. Minute unidentifiable calcined bone fragments have been recovered frequently from these hearths, suggesting bone was burned as fuel, for spiritual purposes, or to keep camps clean. Red ochre, an iron oxide that when reduced to powder forms the basis for a pigment or paint, has been reported associated with several Nenana complex occupations (Goebel and Powers 1989, Phippen 1988:118, Powers and Hoffecker 1990:281). This suggests that red pigment was used to color objects and possibly as body paint. Because little evidence has been found to indicate structures, most sites are believed to have been open-air camps. However, evidence of a possible tent-like structure has been reported from the Walker Road site (Goebel and Powers 1989). Although no structural remains were discovered, the spatial distribution of 160 artifacts around a circular clay-lined hearth dug into the underlying gravels at the base of the loess has been interpreted to be the site of a circular tent approximately 5 meters in diameter.

Most archeologists would agree that the absence of technological traits generally is not an acceptable criterion to use when evaluating the relationship of artifact assemblages. However, it deserves consideration when discussing Nenana complex assemblages, all of which lack microblades. All of the sites presented here under this expanded concept of the Nenana complex have been interpreted as hunting camps by their excavators. It is significant that all these sites contain bifacial lithic artifacts associated with the maintenance and repair of a bifacial projectile point weapon system. Microblades occur in high frequencies in American Paleoarctic tradition sites because they are essential components of composite projectile point systems most commonly associated with Paleoarctic hunting sites. Thus it is probable that functional differences, such as some sites being kill sites while others are camp sites, do not explain the absence of microblades in Nenana complex sites. The difference between bifacially flaked tools and microblade technology may be more than a difference in stoneworking technique. It may signal a fundamental difference in logic for problem solving and therefore a different worldview.

Jim Deetz, a charismatic and innovative archeologist who was on the faculty of Brown University when I was a graduate student there, suggested that there were two contrasting methods for manufacturing artifacts (Deetz 1967:48–49). One was additive and the other was subtractive. In this conceptual framework, the Nenana complex is subtractive while the later American Paleoarctic tradition is additive. The approach to projectile point manufacture by peoples of the Nenana complex is subtractive, because it requires the reduction of a lithic core by flaking away excess rock to create a flaked stone projectile point, or biface. Thus the subtractive approach is characteristic of the Nenana complex.

The American Paleoarctic tradition is a radical and fundamental departure from the technology of the Nenana complex. It represents the additive approach because tool and weapon manufacture in the Paleoarctic tradition is characterized by a technique in which lithic microblades are inset into longitudinal grooves incised in bone, antler, or ivory projectile points. By adding these elements together, technologically sophisticated composite projectile points were manufactured. Burins are believed to be the primary tools used to shape and groove the points, and razor-sharp microblades formed their cutting edge. An interrelated set of lithic artifacts, the burin and microblade, and their associated debitage (microblade cores, core tablets, and burin spalls) reflect this conceptual approach to projectile point manufacture.

These two contrasting and fundamentally different conceptual approaches to tool manufacture suggest that other profound differences in technological and social concepts may have existed between the peoples of the Nenana complex and those of the later American Paleoarctic tradition. The change from the Nenana complex to the American Paleoarctic occurs by circa 10,500 B.P. in eastern Beringia. Because this change is distinctive and abrupt with little or no evidence of technological transition, it may suggest the displacement of one cultural group by another rather than the

The Nenana Complex

evolution or adoption of technology by a single group.

Although this hypothesis is highly speculative, interior Alaska may have been a region repeatedly reoccupied by different cultural groups. The earliest archeological assemblages are ascribed to the Nenana complex, which appears to have been replaced by peoples of the American Paleoarctic tradition, which originated in Asia and expanded eastward, reaching interior Alaska about 10,600 B.P. Evidence from several interior Alaskan sites suggest that the region was once again controlled by later Nenana complex groups between circa 9,500 and 8,500 B.P. Discoveries at the Panguingue Creek (Component II) site may suggest the interior was once again occupied by American Paleoarctic peoples shortly after 8,500 B.P.

CHAPTER 8
PEOPLE BEFORE PALEOINDIANS

 Fairbanks is a relatively small town, and I felt rather ridiculous as I stood, one evening in 1987, at the Fairbanks International Airport just prior to the Alaska Anthropological Association meetings holding a large piece of paper on which I had scrawled "Tom Dillehay." As I waited I encountered at least three acquaintances to whom I had to explain who Tom Dillehay was, why I was there to meet him, and why he was coming to Fairbanks. Living in a small community has both advantages and disadvantages.

As I watched the passengers disembark I could not help but wonder which one would be the archeologist who had spent half of his adult life in South America, spoke excellent Spanish, and was well known both in the villages of the Andean highlands and at the universities of Chile and Peru. I was rather surprised when a tall, well-dressed man whom I guessed to be in his late 30s or early 40s approached and introduced himself. Arctic archeologists tend to be somewhat scruffy. Dillehay was neat, slender, and fashionable. As I got to know him over the next week, I realized that his neat appearance, courteous manner, and physical condition were all traits of an extremely competent individual, and I decided not to hold them against him. Like most archeologists, his attire would have been much different had he arrived to do fieldwork rather than lecture at a university.

Tom Dillehay was as curious about the early archeology of eastern Beringia as I was about that of Monte Verde. During the drive to my house I started to bring him up-to-date on the discovery and subsequent dating of the Nenana complex. I began by explaining that in the 1960s, Hans Jurgen Müller-Beck (1966, 1967), a German archeologist admired for his logic, predicted the general nature of eastern Beringian archeological assemblages based on his analysis of Old World archeological sequences. Müller-Beck provided insights that foreshadowed subsequent discovery of the Nenana complex

Chapter 8

and dating of the American Paleoarctic tradition. He advanced a conceptual framework suggesting that a bifacial technology preceded subsequent microblade technology in eastern Beringia, based on similar sequences documented in the Old World.

Field research during the 1970s and 1980s later documented this sequence and demonstrated the earlier occurrence of the Nenana complex characterized by bifacial stone tools, which was followed by the American Paleoarctic tradition characterized by microblades. However, most prehistorians, and probably Müller-Beck himself, had assumed that the early bifacial tradition in eastern Beringia was like Clovis or its immediate predecessor. Such logic followed the traditional peopling of the New World model, which called for Clovis-like mammoth hunters sweeping out of Asia across the Bering Land Bridge and into the Americas.

Even though the two complexes exhibit a number of similarities, the Nenana complex lacks fluted projectile points, which are the hallmark of the Llano complex. Instead, the Nenana complex is characterized by triangular and teardrop-shaped projectile points or knives. Even more perplexing were the facts that the Llano and Nenana complexes were contemporaneous and both seem to have appeared without precursors in very different parts of North America at almost exactly the same time. Although we knew more by the end of the 1980s than we had 15 years earlier, the situation was in some respects even more confusing.

Having shared this information with Dillehay, I was extremely curious about his excavation and interpretation of Monte Verde. A few years earlier he had published an article in *Scientific American* (Dillehay 1984) describing this site, located in south-central Chile, which was to many North American archeologists a very different and unexpected find and therefore controversial. The site was reported to be approximately 12,500 to 13,000 years old. If the radiocarbon dates were correct, Monte Verde was older than both the Llano and Nenana complexes by at least 1,000 years.

I had been very impressed with the quality of Dillehay's report. The artifacts he illustrated were of human manufacture, and he had even uncovered a human footprint that had been imprinted in soft earth perhaps 13,000–12,500 years ago. He had presented a suite of concordant radiocarbon dates from a primary stratigraphic context, and the associated paleoecological remains supported the dating of the site. These were the very criteria that my friend and colleague Dennis Stanford and other archeologists required to establish the Pleistocene antiquity of archeological remains. From the publication information the site looked good, but I warned myself that so had the publication about the caribou bone flesher from the Old Crow when it had first appeared in the literature. I could not help but wonder if there might be some strange set of natural events that had somehow made Monte Verde seem to be a 13,000–12,500-year-old archeological site when in reality it was younger. Could it

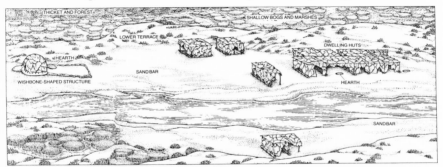

8.1 Reconstruction of 13,000 B.P. settlement at Monte Verde (reproduced with permission from Scientific American *[vol. 251, No. 4] and the author, Dillehay [1984:104–5]).*

possibly result from the fortuitous circumstance of noncultural phenomena such as the redeposition of more recent artifacts with older wood and charcoal? Because I did not know Dillehay, I was not sure I could trust the integrity of his work on this site, which could change dramatically the entire interpretation of the prehistory of the Americas.

The next evening Dillehay presented a lecture at the University of Alaska in which he described an archeological site unlike any I had ever encountered in the Americas. The site had been situated on the margins of a small creek. On the north bank of the creek the foundations of at least 12 rectangular dwellings had been discovered. Surprisingly, they were joined by their walls to form two parallel rows. The excavators had discovered what appeared, and has subsequently been confirmed, to be the remains of animal skin, which they reasoned had been used to cover the huts. Each dwelling contained a brazier, or shallow pit lined with clay to hold hot coals. Stone tools, plant remains, and food stains were concentrated in these braziers. Communal activities at the site were documented by what appeared to be the remains of two large, centrally located hearths about which were found the remains of edible seeds, nuts, fruits, and berries. About 30 meters west of the cluster of dwellings, archeologists found the remains of a wishbone-shaped structure. Here were most of the mastodon bone and stone tools recovered from the site. Along with other floral material the excavators found masticated leaves of the boldo plant, which currently is used by local residents to brew a tea believed to have medicinal value. The unique shape and positioning of the structure along with the associated artifacts suggested to Dillehay that it may have served as a center for dressing meat from large animals, making and using stone tools, and perhaps medicinal practices.

Monte Verde has well-preserved wooden artifacts including mortars, several wooden hafts containing stone scrapers, an assortment of digging sticks, and vast amounts of worked wood and other small objects. Evidence of weapons is documented by grooved stones thought to be used in bolas, or smooth stones for slings, and a pointed lance or spear about 1.5 meters long. Dillehay also found two bifacially flaked stone tools somewhat resembling elongated and rounded projectile points, stone flake cores and flake tools, and worked bone. Even more amazing were the remains of several dwellings with earth and wood foundations and the preservation of a wide variety of plant remains that had been transported to the site by its occupants. Among the preserved plant remains were tubers including the wild potato.

Not only was Monte Verde older than the well-documented big-game hunting sites in North America, but it was also radically different: it was a residential site of some duration, and the economy of its inhabitants was diversified. Based on analysis of the plant remains, it appears to be a year-round settlement with a specialized nonresidential structure. Large and small mammals supplemented a diet that consisted primarily of plant foods.

After his meticulous excavation, Dillehay tested a variety of other hypotheses that might provide alternative explanations for the evidence he had found. His thoroughness was evident as he fielded questions from the university faculty and graduate students after his public lecture at the university. For example, could the charcoal from the clay-lined hearths have been contaminated by older "dead carbon" from coal? The answer was no, because the geology of the region indicated no possible source for this type of contamination. Could trees fortuitously have fallen in such a fashion as to create the false impression of dwellings? No, because the wooden foundations were held into the ground by sharpened wooden stakes, and some were rough-hewn planks. The questions continued to pour forth, and each was courteously answered with sound reasoning supported by solid field data. Someone asked if the stones and mastodon bone in the site could have been derived from a sick mastodon that had ingested the stones at a mineral lick, later died at the site, and had its remains subsequently modified by nonhuman scavengers? At this point the questions suggesting alternative explanations had become so outrageous that Dillehay's interpretation that the Monte Verde site was the result of human occupation seemed incredibly rational. Yet Dillehay had grown accustomed to defending his work before academia. With a little less patience, he explained that the source of the stones at the site could be traced to several different regions and that they had recovered the remains of seven different individual mastodons.

Following Dillehay's presentation I was convinced that Monte Verde was a legitimate 12,500–or 13,000-year-old archeological site. If the same evidence had been presented for an archeological site that was several thousand years younger, no one would have questioned either the age or the nature of the site. In fact, if the site had been younger, many archeologists would have considered it quite dull. In other words, Monte Verde was not being challenged based on standard archeological criteria. The rigorous questioning of the site resulted from the fact that those criteria had identified a site that did not meet our expectations in three ways: its age,

Chapter 8

contents, and location. If new data were presented in the future that did not withstand the test of the fundamental criteria required to evaluate the site, it would be necessary to reevaluate the conclusions. However, as things currently stood, I accepted Tom Dillehay's interpretation of Monte Verde. My fundamental problem was similar to that of many of my colleagues: I could not fit this single, anomalous site into a cohesive theory for the peopling of the Americas.

The following evening Dick Jordan, Tom Dillehay, and I had the opportunity to relax over dinner. Naturally the conversation soon turned to early humans in the Americas. Jordan, who was teaching at Bryn Mawr College in Pennsylvania, brought up the subject of Meadowcroft Rock Shelter. Although Jordan was not a specialist in early human occupation, he was familiar with this important and rather spectacular site, which is located in Pennsylvania and contains a long sequence of cultural occupations. As with many limestone caves and rock shelters, the organic preservation at the site is exceptional. However, the rare discovery of basketry and other organic material culture has been overshadowed by the fact that the earliest cultural occupations were dated by radiocarbon to approximately 16,000–17,000 years ago. Since publications by the site's excavator, Jim Adovasio, and his colleagues began appearing in the late 1970s (Adovasio et al. 1977, 1978), a storm of controversy has raged about the site. As the debate in the academic literature became focused, it seemed that the few lithic artifacts from stratigraphic levels dated to circa 17,000 B.P. were accepted as having been manufactured by humans. The stratigraphy at the site seemed to adequately define and separate cultural occupations. However, the absence of Pleistocene fauna associated with the artifacts was viewed by some researchers to imply that these levels might be Holocene in age. Secondly, it was suggested that the radiocarbon dates from the lowest levels might indicate contamination by coal or other older organics. Adovasio and his colleagues (1980) had addressed these issues through an interdisciplinary research effort, and, as best as I could judge based on these reports, the site, like Monte Verde, seemed to meet the criteria required by archeological science.

People before Paleoindians

Our discussion then touched on a variety of sites discovered over the years that had been proposed as Pleistocene age sites. These sites in both North and South America had been presented and discussed in publications by researchers such as Alan Bryan (1978, 1986) who are proponents for the lengthy antiquity of humans in the Americas. This list was extensive, yet critics have challenged each of the sites as either improperly dated or misinterpreted, or for some other reason the dates remain equivocal.

I reflected that this was clearly true for the sites from eastern Beringia. Each site, assemblage of artifacts, or proposed archeological complex in eastern Beringia reportedly older than 12,000 B.P. that had been proposed over the past 50 years either had been disproven or remained equivocal. In fact, I was one of the researchers who had been skeptical of these data and had found flaws in the analysis of reported early archeological sites. Several colleagues and I had revisited an alleged Pleistocene site near Chinitna Bay, Alaska, and discovered that the site, if it had existed at all, could not be Pleistocene in age based on the local geology (Thorson et al. 1980).

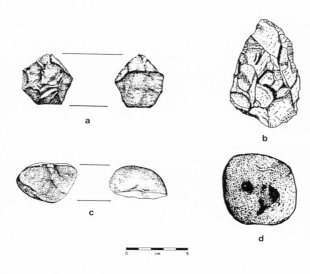

8.2 Artifacts from the 33,000 B.P. levels at Monte Verde: (a) percussion-split basalt pebble; (b) unifacially flaked basalt core; (c) percussion flake made of basalt; and (d) edge-battered basalt cobble (reproduced with permission from Nature *[vol. 332, 10 March 1988] and the primary author, Dillehay [1988: figure 2, p. 151]).*

Chapter 8

A few years later along with my friend and colleague George Smith (Dixon and Smith 1986), I discovered that the "broken dog canines" cited as Pleistocene cultural evidence in the Trail Creek Caves were really deciduous bear teeth. My research along the Alaskan portion of the Porcupine River and the excavation of several caves in that area led me to question the age, associations, and cultural origin of proposed artifacts from the Old Crow area and Blue Fish Caves based on taphonomic evidence and cave geomorphology (Dixon 1984). My archeological experiences in the north had placed me on the conservative side of the debate; it seemed to me that there existed no firm evidence for humans in eastern Beringia prior to 11,500 B.P.

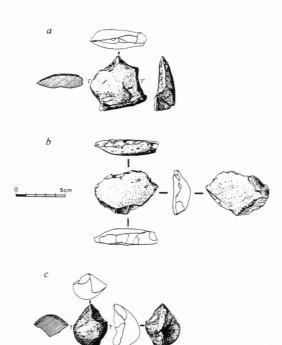

8.3 *Possible Pleistocene age artifacts recovered from Pedra Furada, Brazil, ca. 32,000* B.P.: *(a and b) possible retouched flakes, and (c) possible flake core (reproduced with permission from* Nature *[vol. 321, 19 June 1986] and the author, Guidan [1986:771]).*

People before Paleoindians

Our conversation turned to Dillehay's lecture on Monte Verde. He had mentioned briefly a deeper and possibly much older cultural occupation at Monte Verde, but he had been extremely cautious and stated that the analysis of this material was not yet complete. He explained to us that he had found what appeared to be 26 stone artifacts, the majority of which had been naturally fractured but culturally used. Several showed clear evidence of cultural modification by percussion flaking. He had found them clustered about concentrations of charcoal in three distinct hearth-like basins. Two radiocarbon dates from these hearth-like features indicated that they were approximately 33,000 years old!

Jordan and I both began to bombard him with questions. Although Dillehay did not publish this information until a year later (Dillehay and Collins 1988), he was more than willing to respond to our questions. Could the lithics have been redeposited in the site? No, there was nothing in the stratigraphy to suggest this, and the fact that they were dispersed about the hearth-like features supported his interpretation. Could the artifacts have worked down through the sediment from the 13,000-year-old occupation? No, although they were stratigraphically below the earlier occupation, they were about 70 meters to the north. Could they have resulted from some unexplained natural phenomena that could have deposited rock and charcoal along the stream margin some 33,000 years ago? Although possible, no such mechanism was known. Further, more than 250 square meters of this surface had been exposed, and the artifacts and charcoal had been recovered only from this one locale.

The previous year a French archeologist, N. Guidon, whom I had not met, published a startling article. She was attempting to date prehistoric art that was well known from a series of Brazilian rock shelters. It is difficult for archeologists to determine the age of paintings on cave walls and on vertical rock surfaces because these artifacts are not buried in the ground with associated organics as are most lost or discarded tools. One way to address this problem is to attempt to discover a fragment of the cave wall with part of the art preserved on its surface buried in the sediment on the floor. If the stratigraphic level from which the fragment has been found can be radiocarbon-dated, then researchers can safely assume that the painting on the wall is as old as, or older than, the level from which the fragment was recovered. Not only had she been successful in employing this method, but the radiocarbon determinations indicated that the level from which the fragment came was approximately 17,000 years old (Guidon and Delibrias 1986).

The site is called Boqueirao do Sitio da Pedra Furada, which English-speaking archeologists soon shortened to simply Pedra Furada. The ancient rock art was by itself an amazing discovery because if the dating was correct, it would be among the oldest known art in the world. The French researchers also reported an impressive suite of 17 radiocarbon dates beginning about 6,000 years ago and extending back to 32,000 years ago! The site had six stratigraphic levels, the oldest of which contained stone tools similar to those that Tom Dillehay had discovered from the lower level at Monte Verde. The deposits appeared to be mostly sands, silts, pebbles, and cobbles, which suggested that they had been transported by the adjacent stream. My experience indicated that sediments transported by flowing water can create difficult problems for archeological interpretation. For example, wood and other organics burned in forest fires can be transported by streams and deposited in these sediments. Furthermore, rivers and streams can tumble and fracture rocks in such a way as to resemble artifacts made by humans. While I did not discount the evidence from Pedra Furada, it was important for this site to be reported in greater detail if it was to be properly assessed.

It was uncanny that two different researchers working independently in different parts of South America had found similar types of stone tools dating to approximately the same time period. In the 12,500–13,000 B.P. occupation of Monte Verde, approximately 90% of the stone tools were naturally fractured or unfractured stones picked up and used by the inhabitants (Dillehay 1984). Ironically, if these tools had not been recovered within the context of an archeological site containing excellent organic preservation, they probably would have gone unreported or, had they been reported, certainly their association with humans would have been questioned.

People before Paleoindians

Did the data from Pedra Furada and Monte Verde indicate that by 33,000 years ago human groups were established in South America, already well adapted to different environments and resources? Did the vast array of other sites regarded by most prehistorians to be equivocal, but certainly possible, evidence of humans in the Americas prior to 12,000 B.P. support continued occupation until the end of the Pleistocene? Did these sites indicate a wide variety of adaptations over vast areas of North and South America continuing until the firmly documented remains of the Nenana and Llano complexes were encountered in the archeological record? We lacked the answers to these questions. My knowledge of eastern Beringian prehistory led me to postulate that if there were archeological evidence older than the Nenana complex, either it had not yet been found or it had been recovered but not recognized. Could it be possible that humans had somehow bypassed or skirted eastern Beringia during their migration to the New World?

* * * * * * *

Tom Dillehay had been invited to Fairbanks by the Alaska Quaternary Center, a group of scientists from a variety of disciplines at the University of Alaska who share research interests in climate, geology, and prehistory throughout the Pleistocene. Dillehay's visit had been timed to coincide with the Alaska Anthropological Association meetings so that a greater number of Alaskan scientists would have the opportunity to become familiar with him and his research.

At the same time, the Alaska Anthropological Association had invited Brian Fagan to be its guest speaker at the annual meeting. Fagan, an excellent writer, is a master at synthesizing vast amounts of archeological information and presenting it in a manner that imparts to the public and professionals alike an accurate sense of the life of prehistoric peoples and the great accomplishments of mankind. Prior to his visit to Alaska, he had published a book entitled *The Great Journey* (Fagan 1987), in which he reviewed the earliest archeological data from the Americas. In this excellent book he adopted the conservative perspective that there exists no

Chapter 8

unequivocal data supporting human occupation of the Americas prior to circa 12,000 B.P. and that the first Americans entered the New World by crossing Beringia.

While Fagan was in Fairbanks he presented lectures to packed auditoriums and large luncheon audiences. It was ironic that hundreds, possibly thousands, of people turned out to hear him lecture, while at the same time Tom Dillehay was talking to small groups of academics and presenting data contrary to Fagan's lectures. Though consensus provides the security and comfort most people require, it frequently may not reflect the truth. Fortunately, most scientific debates are not subject to final resolution by popular vote.

CHAPTER 9

NEW DISCOVERIES

 During my previous visit to Victoria, Tom Loy had told me that he had accepted a position at Australia National University in Canberra, Australia's capital. We would have to complete our research before he left Canada later in the summer. In addition, I had been asked to serve as acting director of our museum for the next year. If we failed to complete the research in the immediate future, these other duties and Tom Loy's departure to Australia would make it impossible to complete this project, to which we had already devoted considerable effort. After the spring semester was finished and my teaching responsibilities were over, I planned to travel to Victoria again and bring to a close this episode in the quest for the origins of the first Americans.

Early in the summer of 1987 we resumed our meticulous and tedious efforts in Victoria. Just as we were fully engaged in the research, Loy's lab was abruptly closed without notice. One moment we were in the middle of our research and the next we were standing on the street holding in our hands almost the entire collection of fluted projectile points from eastern Beringia, rolls of undeveloped film, and small, sealed vials containing the residue extracts!

The next day I changed my airplane reservations and returned to Fairbanks, bringing with me the collection of fluted points and our lab data sheets, residue samples, and film. In spite of the disregard for our ongoing research by the British Columbia Provincial Museum, I was more determined than ever to complete this project. I began making arrangements for laboratory facilities at the University of Alaska and to bring Loy to Fairbanks.

To offset this bad fortune, upon my return I learned that Dick Jordan had accepted a position as chairman of the University of Alaska anthropology program in Fairbanks. Also, I was delighted to learn that Dennis Stanford would spend the spring semester of the

Chapter 9

next academic year at the University of Alaska as visiting professor of quaternary sciences, sponsored by our Alaska Quaternary Center.

Later that summer Tom Loy traveled to Alaska. With the assistance of colleagues at the university, we obtained the use of laboratory facilities necessary to complete the research. We began work almost as soon as Loy arrived and continued until we were satisfied that we had learned what we could from the residues. Our microscopic examination of the surfaces of the fluted projectile points eliminated 15 of the 36 specimens from further analysis because no residues were observed or they were contaminated or obscured by casting compounds, ink, or other substances. Blood residues were observed on all of the remaining specimens; however, in 6 cases they were too small for extraction and analysis. Our research proceeded on the remaining 15 fluted points with sufficient blood residue for analysis. The Ames Hemastix documented, and dot blot tests confirmed, blood residues on all 15 of these specimens.

Microscopy verified both the Ames Hemastix and dot blot tests on 12 of the points (80% of the cases) through identification of red blood cells. Samples were selected for isoelectric focusing from 4 (26%) of the 15 projectile points because they contained sufficient residue for this as well as the other tests. The results of the IEF analysis were determined by statistically comparing the similarity of the residues to those of known species. This analysis indicated that mammoth blood was probably preserved on 1 of the 4 projectile points, a conclusion later verified by hemoglobin crystallization and the observation of red blood cells of 9.4–9.6 microns in diameter. Isoelectric focusing further suggested that on the 3 remaining specimens the blood of 2 or more species had been preserved. Hemoglobin crystallization subsequently verified this in all 3 cases. All these tests demonstrated that the residues were primarily composed of blood; each independent technique produced results consistent with the other tests.

As we systematically worked our way through the assemblage, the analysis began to form a pattern. A picture emerged that seemed to indicate that all of the projectile points with preserved residues suitable for analysis had been used for big-game hunting. Hemoglo-

Site	Catalog Number	RBC Diameter	Mammoth	Bison	Sheep	Bear	Caribou	Musk Ox	Comment
Batza Tena	Rklg 30:160						X		
Batza Tena area	Rklg 30:323						X		
Driftwood Creek	Uncataloged						X		
Girls Hill	UA74-27-228	10.8	X				X		A
Girls Hill	UA74-27-1256						X		
Girls Hill	UA74-27-6485	4.8	X	X					B
Hanks Hill	UA76-203							X	
Kugururok River	423535	4.5 - 5.0 10 - 11	X			X			
Lisburne	UA78-80-1105	9.4 - 9.6	X						
Lisburne	UA78-80-633	7.2 4.8	X		X	X			
Old Crow Area	70-K-A4/1	5.4					X		
Point Site	UA78-77-01		X						
Putu	UA70-84-73						X		
Teshekpuk Lake	UA78-224-1	4.8							C
Utukok River	391806	7.2 4.9		X			X		

9.1 *The results of the residue analysis of the fluted projectile points from eastern Beringia, summarized by site, catalog number, observed red cell size, and identification of species of origin using hemoglobin crystallization. Red blood cell (RBC) diameters are in microns (mu); x indicates the species crystal observed. Comment A: soapy residue, most likely a parting compound used for casting. Comment B: fragment of unidentified hair in residue observed during high magnification microscopy of the tool surface. Comment C: cholesterol crystals observed during high-magnification microscopy of the tool surface.*

Chapter 9

9.2 Some of the fluted projectile points analyzed in this study: (a) Batza Téna RkIg-31:60; (b) Utukok, 391806; (c) Putu, uncataloged; (d) Putu, UA70-84-73: (e) Girls Hill, UA74-27-6485; (f) Girls Hill, UA74-27-1256; (g) RkIg-31:120; (h)Batza Téna, RIIg-47-13; (i) Driftwood, uncataloged; (j) Teshekpuk Lake, UA78-224-1; (k) Kugururok River, 423535; (l) Lisburne, UA78-80-633; (m) Batza Téna, RkIg-43:1; (n) Hanks Hill, UA76-203; (o) Old Crow, EF 8884:1896; (p) Old Crow, 70-K-A4/1; (q) Girls Hill, UA74-27-228.

bin crystallization identified 6 different species when compared with the control blood crystals: 5 residues produced mammoth *(Mammuthus primigenius)* crystals, 2 had bison *(Bison)*, 2 had sheep *(Ovis dalli)*, 1 had bear *(Ursus arctos)*, 1 had musk ox *(Ovibos moschatus)* and 6 had caribou *(Rangifer tarandus)*. Of the projectile points, 5 had residues from more than one species: 1 was a mix of sheep and bear; 1 was caribou and bison; 2 were mixtures of mammoth and bison; and 1 was caribou and sheep. Because the subsistence strategy of the Llano complex was based on big-game hunting, these data indicated that the function of the northern fluted points was consistent with the function of fluted projectile points to the south.

Even more important was documenting the association of mammoth with fluted projectile points from eastern Beringia. This strongly suggested that these points should be classified with other North American Paleoindian artifact assemblages based on their mutual association with extinct fauna and apparent specialization in big-game hunting. Although further research was needed, we felt our analysis was significant because fluted projectile points from eastern Beringia had not been directly linked with specific fauna prior to our study.

The chronological placement of the assemblage of fluted points remained equivocal, but the occurrence of *Mammuthus primigenius* indicated a late Pleistocene or early Holocene age. On the basis of these data I felt we could reject the hypothesis that fluted projectile points were invented later and independently in eastern Beringia and that they bear no historical relationship to the Llano complex. However, these data alone do not demonstrate a northern or southern origin for the Llano complex, nor do they confirm the overkill hypothesis of Pleistocene extinctions, which attributes extinction to human predation (Martin 1967, 1973, 1982, 1984; Mosimann and Martin 1975). Accurate dating of these artifact types was required to further evaluate their age and utility in explaining Pleistocene extinctions in eastern Beringia.

Though I had been able to formulate the research problem, assemble the specimens and tissue samples, and provide basic laboratory assistance, I lacked the technical expertise to fully understand the analytical procedures and underlying biochemistry. After spending many hours looking through the microscope with Loy's patient guidance, I could recognize groups of crystals that were alike. Although I accepted Loy's identification of them, the truth of the matter was that I could not tell whether these groups of crystals were hemoglobin crystals. Procedures such as isoelectric

Chapter 9

focusing were foreign to me and produced results that could not be verified by the naked eye, much less by someone who knew little about biochemistry. Suppose there was some fundamental flaw in what we were doing that made the results of the various tests appear to verify each other when in reality they did not?

The only solution I could find for this personal dilemma was to attempt to publish our methods and results. This would place this experimental research squarely before other scientists who could evaluate both the methods and conclusion. Furthermore, Loy and I both felt that it was important to get archeologists and other scientists to begin thinking about this type of research. Even if our original work should prove to be flawed in some respect, the very fact that others would conduct the research necessary to discover our mistakes would advance this type of analysis. A little controversy can frequently stimulate research interest and accelerate progress.

Loy's research approach drew upon recent techniques in biochemistry which we used to address a long-standing archeological problem. It clearly underscored the importance of museum collections and the need for sound curatorial procedures that guard against contamination, destruction, or modification of specimens as they are received from the field. The techniques Loy applied to the fluted point problem were pioneering, and we fully realized that they eventually would be replaced by less subjective analytical tests exhibiting greater precision and resolution. As residue analysis becomes increasingly refined, the results of early experiments such as ours must be verified. However, we felt that it was important to begin to build a body of literature from which others could draw and to expand general awareness of these types of research among archeologists and museum professionals.

Loy and I finished preparation of a manuscript that presented the results of our research at about 1:00 in the morning, and a few hours later I drove him to the airport. He would fly from Fairbanks to Victoria and begin the long journey to Australia. We had decided to submit the manuscript to *Science,* which is the most prestigious and possibly most conservative scientific journal in the United States.

New Discoveries

After Loy left, I went through the laborious task of editing and formatting our article to meet the requirements of the journal, and soon it was in the mail. About two weeks later I received word that our manuscript had passed the first level of screening by the board of reviewing editors and that it had been sent on to specialists within the field for technical review. After two months had passed, we had received no further word from the journal, so I decided to call the editorial office. The following week I received a letter from the editor stating that although the reviewers had unanimously

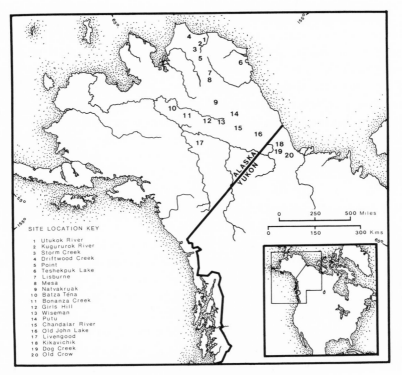

9.3 The northern distribution of fluted point locales, suggesting the possible late persistence of mammoth in northern eastern Beringia.

Chapter 9

recommended publication, they would not publish the article. The crux of the issue was that although all expressed confidence that the residues had been correctly identified, there was a degree of subjectivity in the methods that lacked definitive and absolute proof. With Loy in Australia setting up a new laboratory and with my additional responsibilities, I realized that it would be a long time before we could coordinate a response to the reviewers' comments and resubmit the manuscript for publication. Two years passed before Loy and I came together again to finish this work.

* * * * * * *

Over the course of the following winter Dennis Stanford was a frequent and welcome visitor to my office. As a visiting professor of quaternary science he was taking a break from his usual duties as curator of Paleoindian archeology at the Smithsonian Institution. We would discuss archeological issues over coffee at my office in the mornings or later in the day over stronger beverages with Dick Jordan. Although Stanford had been aware of our residue research, I brought him up-to-date on the results shortly after his arrival in Fairbanks. I explained how I had originally hypothesized that mammoth residues would not be preserved on these points because I thought mammoth would have been extinct in eastern Beringia by the time these points were used in the region. However, the association of fluted projectile points from eastern Beringia with the blood residues of *Mammuthus primigenius* left little doubt that a predator/prey relationship existed between humans and this extinct species.

Stanford had excavated mammoth kill sites in the southwestern United States, so the idea of mammoth associated with these early archeological complexes seemed less unlikely to him than it did to me. The sites where fluted projectile points had been found in eastern Beringia are largely restricted to the northern areas of Alaska and Canada's Yukon Territory. Furthermore, the residue analysis indicated that the peoples who used these artifacts shared a similar economic system based on hunting mammoth and other large mammals with the Llano complex. Why were the points largely

New Discoveries

restricted to these northern areas of eastern Beringia, and why had they never been discovered in western Beringia?

The restricted distribution of the Northern Paleoindian tradition may have been a result of the economic base utilized by these people. The northern distribution of these sites, coupled with the results of the residue analysis, suggests that mammoth may have survived into the very late Pleistocene or early Holocene in northern areas of eastern Beringia. If this was the case, environmental conditions favorable to their survival and similar to those of the Pleistocene may have persisted later in this region than in other regions of North America.

If I stuck to the position that the northern fluted projectile points were younger than those to the south, only two possible conclusions followed: either mammoths survived much later in eastern Beringia than anywhere else in the Americas, or our identification of mammoth residue on the northern points was not correct. Assuming our identifications were correct, it seemed plausible that mammoth were hunted about 11,000 years ago by peoples of the Nenana complex. Although the proboscidean tusk fragments from the Broken Mammoth and Mead sites may have been scavenged from the landscape by the sites' occupants, they also may have been procured from animals that had been actively hunted, and mammoths may have still been living in central eastern Beringia 11,000 years ago. If the blood residue analyses are correct, mammoth evidently persisted as late as 9,500 years ago at the Jay Creek Ridge site.

Although not conclusive, data were beginning to emerge that implied that mammoth may have survived later in eastern Beringia than in other parts of the world. Dennis Stanford fully realized that we were pushing at the edges of our discipline. He encouraged us to address the reviewer comments and submit the manuscript for publication in another journal. I knew that he was correct and that the alternative was to suppress potentially significant knowledge for fear of rejection or further criticism. With this encouragement, I began making plans to go to Australia to work again with Tom Loy to bring our research to publication.

Although the data were still ambiguous, they suggested to me that fluted point technology had spread northward to eastern Beringia following partition of continental ice. The evidence from Monte Verde, Meadowcroft Rock Shelter, and possibly Pedra Furada supported the arrival of humans in the Americas and their dispersal prior to 12,000 years ago. If these interpretations were correct, humans would necessarily have reached areas south of the continental glaciers prior to their coalescence or moved southward along the fringe of the northwest coast of North America during the last glacial.

CHAPTER 10

SYNTHESIS

 In the fall of 1989 Dennis Stanford departed on his long overland return trip to the Smithsonian Institution. Soon after he left, I applied for sabbatical leave from the university for the following academic year. My plan was to complete a number of projects that always seemed to be set aside for the more urgent matters that arise in a museum on a daily basis. High on my list of unfinished projects was bringing our research on the fluted point residues to publication. Later that winter I was delighted to learn that I had been granted sabbatical leave for a full 12-month period. As soon as my leave started in the summer of 1990 I began my synthesis of the late Pleistocene and early Holocene prehistory of eastern Beringia.

Synthesis is an ongoing process in archeological science. It necessitates moving from the security of well-known small-scale phenomena within restricted areas into the less secure realm of defining patterns of information derived by many researchers from many different archeological sites from diverse regions. Synthesis is required periodically to modify existing interpretations or to offer new interpretations to accommodate new discoveries, the application of new methods, and the progress of ongoing research. During the past 20 years new knowledge of the prehistory of eastern Beringia includes defining the age and geographic distribution of the American Paleoarctic tradition, discovery of the Nenana complex, and new methods in residue analysis identifying the blood of Pleistocene mammals on fluted projectile points. These developments necessitated a new synthesis, placing this progress within a structured framework that would not only make sense out of the details but also serve as the foundation for continuing research.

A regional synthesis of eastern Beringia should provide a cohesive presentation consistent with the regional data. Furthermore, it must be articulated with information from adjacent regions and general advances in world archeology. This requires looking at

115

Chapter 10

patterns between individual sites and lumping or separating artifact assemblages based on their similarities, dissimilarities, and age. It also requires imagination and speculation to bridge gaps where there may be no data or where the data are so meager that they may only hint at a pattern. It is imagination and speculation that provide the basis for hypotheses that may be tested against future discoveries or interpretations of the archeological record. Because synthesis requires speculation it is important for researchers to recognize where the data end and speculation or imagination begins.

Conclusions drawn from my synthesis challenge the popular land bridge theory of human dispersal in the New World. The old hypothesis postulates that humans first entered North America from Asia during the Pleistocene when sea level was lower and Asia and North America were joined, forming a single continent. Though the existence of the Bering Land Bridge and its potential usefulness in human migration are not disputed, the land bridge as the required or sole mechanism for human travel from Asia to the New World is not realistic. I looked for interpretations as I synthesized the contemporary data. Three prehistoric cultural traditions have been documented in eastern Beringia that are important to understanding the colonization of the New World. These traditions are the Nenana complex, the American Paleoarctic tradition, and the Northern Paleoindian tradition.

*　*　*　*　*　*　*

The earliest firmly dated archeological assemblage in eastern Beringia is ascribed to the Nenana complex, which has been documented at several sites in interior Alaska. This bifacial industry lacked microblades and emphasized the manufacture of triangular and teardrop-shaped bifaces. Large game including elk, bison, and sheep were hunted; however, sites with well-preserved faunal remains suggest that small game, waterfowl, and salmon may have been more important. Although there is no conclusive proof of mammoth predation, mammoth ivory from two sites and highly experimental blood residue analysis of projectile points from the Jay Ridge site suggest that mammoth may have been hunted or their

Synthesis

remains scavenged. The earliest radiometric dates indicate that this tradition appeared in eastern Beringia sometime before 11,300 B.P. and may have persisted throughout the Birch interval circa 8,500 B.P.

The Nenana complex is followed by the American Paleoarctic tradition in interior Alaska. The American Paleoarctic tradition is first documented in the Americas by about 10,600 B.P. It is characterized by wedge-shaped microblade cores; larger blade cores; blades; microblades; core tablets; elongate bifaces; concave-, convex-, and straight-based projectile points or knives; burins struck on flakes and blades; burin spalls; scrapers; spokeshaves; and abraders. American Paleoarctic tradition sites have been documented over a vast area extending from the arctic coastal plain of northern Alaska as far south as the state of Washington in the Pacific Northwest.

The highly distinctive and different nature of this tool kit suggests that it may represent the remains of a cultural group different from the Nenana complex. It persists in time throughout the Birch interval and may be regarded as a co-tradition with the Nenana complex during that time period. Numerous sites documented along the northern Pacific rim of North America between 9,000 and 6,500 B.P. demonstrate a pronounced maritime adaptation in sites along the coast.

Although the data are extremely fragmentary, they suggest that an earlier underlying bifacial industry may have preceded the Paleoarctic tradition in western and southeastern Alaska as it did in the interior. Between 10,000 and 11,000 B.P. the coast of western Alaska lay farther offshore than its present position. At this time early American Paleoarctic hunters may have already begun the process of adaptation to intensive maritime exploitation in response to a surge in marine productivity resulting from the newly established connection of the Arctic and Pacific oceans at the end of the Pleistocene. Coastal sites dating to this time are difficult to find, because they are likely to be under water today or destroyed by rising sea level.

Sites such as Dry Creek (Powers and Hoffecker 1990) in central interior Alaska and the Gallagher Flint Station (Dixon 1975) in northern Alaska indicate that American Paleoarctic populations were in place in interior areas and probably along the coast by at least circa

Chapter 10

10,500 B.P. It is clear that the origins of the American Paleoarctic tradition and probably many subsequent technological innovations are derived from Asia. Larsen (1968b) suggests that technological continuity between later microblade cultures of the Arctic Small Tool tradition, which flourished in eastern Beringia between circa 4,200 and 1,200 B.P. can be traced through the direct historic approach to contemporary Inuit populations (Anderson 1968). The repeated association of artifact types indicate technological continuity between the American Paleoarctic tradition and the Arctic Small Tool tradition and suggests that the American Paleoarctic tradition may provide the technological base from which subsequent Inuit and Aleut cultures developed. The technological tradition may be viewed as the last major diffusion of technology or movement of peoples out of Asia into eastern Beringia and probably occurred by circa 11,000 or 10,500 years ago.

The age and origin of the Northern Paleoindian tradition in eastern Beringia is uncertain. The Northern Paleoindian tradition is defined by a series of archeological sites and isolated finds characterized by fluted projectile points. Although bone has not been preserved in these sites, an economic pattern based on big-game hunting, including mammoth, is indicated from the results of experimental blood residue analysis. These experimental data suggest that the Northern Paleoindian tradition is both technologically and economically related to the Paleoindian tradition in more southern areas of North America.

Fluted projectile points have not been discovered in Siberia. It is presumed that fluted projectile points characteristic of this tradition were invented in the Americas. Because northern fluted projectile points have been found only in contexts that are not datable by standard dating techniques, we must infer their age from other information. One factor suggesting that they are younger in the north is that typologically the northern examples of this tradition bear greater similarity to the younger Folsom rather than the earlier Clovis points of the American Southwest. One limiting factor in the spread, either north or south, of these points is the availability of an ice-free corridor between the continental glaciers in central North America during the Pleistocene. The geology and paleoecology of

Synthesis

this region indicates that it was not until circa 11,500 B.P. that the continental ice had melted sufficiently to create an ice-free corridor. In this corridor no archeological sites have been documented that

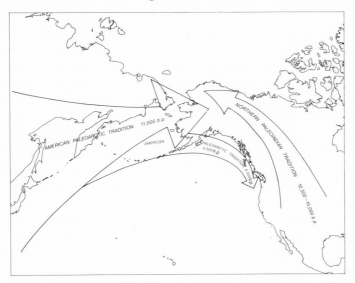

10.1 Northeastern Asia and northwestern North America, illustrating early Holocene distribution of the American Paleoarctic tradition and probable distribution of the Northern Paleoindian tradition.

are older than 11,000 B.P. In summary, the existing evidence suggests that this tradition developed south of the continental ice and that fluted point technology spread northward possibly between 10,500 and 10,000 B.P., following partition of the continental ice. When absolute dating techniques firmly document the age of this tradition in the north, it may be necessary to revise this chronology. These early archeological sequences from eastern Beringia must be placed into the context of data from other areas of the world, including North and South America and western Beringia.

Fladmark (1979, 1983) has postulated human migration southward along the northwest coast of North America during the Pleistocene. He suggests that with the use of watercraft, humans gradually could have colonized unglaciated refugia as well as areas along the continental shelf exposed by lower sea level during the Pleis-

Chapter 10

tocene. Geologic and paleoecologic studies (Blaise et al. 1990, Bobrowsky et al. 1990) document deglaciation and the existence of ice-free areas throughout major coastal areas of British Columbia by 13,000 B.P. (Blaise et al. 1990:294). Although we have no direct evidence of watercraft, we are not unreasonable in assuming its existence. This possibility is reinforced by the fact that Australia, which was not connected to Asia by a land bridge during the Pleistocene, was colonized by at least 40,000 B.P. (Schutler 1983), presumably by people with watercraft.

If a coastal migration with the use of watercraft took place, the initial human populations may have spread southward with great rapidity. We would expect considerable cultural diversity to have developed rapidly as people adapted to local economic resources along the west coast of the Americas. In relatively brief periods of time, different subsistence and settlement patterns may have developed to time the harvest of food resources specific to various ecological areas. Fladmark (1986) indicates that even primitive watercraft could travel the entire west coast of North and South America in ten years. Although this does not imply that both continents were settled in ten years' time, it does underscore the comparatively rapid rate at which peoples could have spread along the west coast of the Americas.

The documentation and accurate dating of a series of Paleoarctic sites along the northeastern Pacific rim during the 1970s and 1980s led Jordan (1992) to suggest classifying these sites under the term Maritime Paleoarctic tradition, based on their obvious marine economic orientation and the fact that they exhibit the major typological traits defining the Paleoarctic tradition. These sites range in age between circa 9,000 and 7,500 B.P. and are distributed from the Aleutian Islands along the Gulf of Alaska southward along the northwest coast of North America until they reach their southern limit in the state of Washington by circa 6,500 B.P. (Dumond 1980:990).

Although the evidence is fragmentary, early bifacial industries may have preceded Paleoarctic industries along the northwest coast as Jordan (1992) suggests. This sequence would indicate that an early spread of peoples bearing a bifacial technology may have preceded the subsequent spread of the Paleoarctic tradition throughout

Synthesis

northwestern North America. Goebel and Powers (1990; Goebel et al. 1991) have suggested that the Nenana complex bears greater technological similarity to Clovis assemblages from the more southern areas of North America than to Paleoarctic assemblages. With the exception of projectile point forms, these assemblages are similar in many respects. Because they are contemporaneous, Goebel and his associates (1991) suggest that they may both be derived from a common technological tradition that predates both the Clovis and Nenana complexes and possibly represents the first humans to enter the Americas.

Only two archeological sites from the region east of the Verkhoyansk Range in western Beringia are known to date to the late Pleistocene (Michael 1984, Powers 1973). These are the site of Berelekh, located on a tributary of the Indigirka River near the Arctic Ocean (dated to circa 13,000 B.P.), which apparently contains bifacial projectile point fragments but lacks microblades (Mochanov 1977, cited in Powers and Hoffecker 1989:283, 284) and the better-known and -described prehistoric settlement at Ushki Lake in central Kamchatka. Horizon VII at Ushki I has been radiocarbon-dated to circa 14,000 B.P. and contains a bifacial lithic industry consisting primarily of stemmed points. More recently the age of Level VII at Ushki I has been revised; Level VII is now believed to be circa 11,500 B.P. based on several radiocarbon dates (A. V. Lozhkin, personal communication). According to the site's excavator, Dikov, Horizon VII lacks microblades and is superimposed by Horizon VI, which contains microblades and dates to circa 10,500 B.P. (Dikov 1977, 1979 cited in Powers 1989; Dikov and Titov 1984).

Horizons VII and VI at Ushki Lake may be important, for they may demonstrate the same sequence that has been documented in eastern Beringia, which is a bifacial industry lacking microblades followed by later microblade-bearing cultures. Ushki Lake is located on the peninsula of Kamchatka, which during the late Pleistocene was connected by the Beringian continental shelf with North America. This could indicate that prior to 11,500 B.P., peoples employing a bifacial lithic industry were established in western Beringia and already had expanded eastward along the southern margins of Beringia and southward along the northwest coast of North America.

Chapter 10

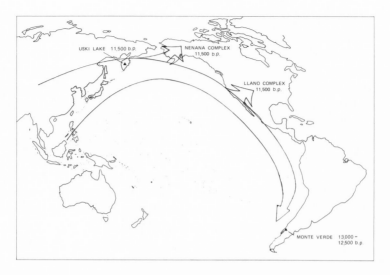

10.2 The Pacific Rim, showing the hypothetical movement of a generalized bifacial stone industry along the coasts of the Americas, ca. 14,000 B.P.

This model suggests that prior to 11,500 B.P. and possibly as early as 14,000–13,000 B.P., peoples had spread south along the west coasts of North and South America. This dispersal is postulated to have occurred as the last glacial drew to a close and may have been in response to rapid sea level rise, which disrupted coastal environmental settings and displaced human groups on the Asian coasts. Using rather conservative mathematical modeling of human population growth, Mosimann and Martin (1975) demonstrated that the continents of both North and South America could have been fully populated within 1,000 years. Archeological traces of this expansion should not be expected to look alike, but as Dillehay (1988) and Meltzer (1989) have suggested should reflect a wide variety of adaptations ranging from the subarctic to the tropics in marine and adjacent terrestrial systems. This suggests that considerable regional diversity may have evolved by 12,000 or 13,000 B.P. Post-Pleistocene sea level rise may have left much of the evidence of this postulated movement either submerged along the western continental shelves of the Americas or destroyed by rising sea level.

With the information available today from archeological sites

Synthesis

discovered in recent decades and calling upon what we know about late Pleistocene environments and habitat, we can postulate a different picture of the peopling of the New World than was possible 20 years ago. What follows is a speculative picture that attempts to accommodate the data from other parts of the Americas with the current understanding of the prehistory of eastern Beringia. As additional discoveries are made and new data and research methods become available, the reevaluation of this speculative framework will be necessary.

The majority of the world's population has lived in the past, and continues to live, along the coasts. Prior to the development of agriculture most inland areas could not support large populations. As sea level began to rise rapidly shortly before 14,000 years ago it probably triggered massive movement and ecological readjustment of the human population inhabiting the Asian Pacific rim. At that time this may have been one of the most densely populated areas of the world. Populations in the Asian north probably began to move eastward, employing the use of watercraft along the southern margins of Beringia into the New World. Rapid expansion may have been possible, with a vast array of environmental settings, economic strategies, technological adaptations, and settlement patterns presenting themselves. The site of Monte Verde indicates that by 13,000–12,500 B.P., human groups probably were already adapted to the noncoastal environment of South America. The sedentary character of settlement at this site reflects an economic strategy from which subsequent Andean cultures may have developed.

By circa 11,500 B.P., human groups had moved into interior areas of the North American continent and developed unique subsistence strategies. The Nenana complex represents human adaptation in the subarctic of eastern Beringia, and the Llano complex represents a different but contemporaneous adaptation in temperate regions of interior North America. Following partition of continental ice, the Llano complex spread northward into eastern Beringia, where remnant populations of mammoth and bison persisted in northern areas. The Llano and Nenana complexes may be examples of groups that gradually adapted to less productive inland habitats as glaciers retreated and the climate ameliorated. Although possibly sharing

Chapter 10

a common technological origin, each reflects different environmental and technological adaptations to different ecological and environmental conditions.

Fluted projectile points do not occur in Asia. The spread of this uniquely American technology and subsistence strategy from more southern areas of North America northwest into eastern Beringia stopped before it reached the Bering Sea coast. Peoples of the American Paleoarctic tradition probably controlled vast areas of eastern Beringia, including the coastal areas of the Bering and Chukchi seas. By this time they were possibly already adapting to exploitation of the marine resources of the Bering and Chukchi seas, which were enriched by the flooding of the Bering Land Bridge. It is from the technological base of the American Paleoarctic tradition and this early post-Pleistocene environmental adaptation that Inuit and Aleut cultures may have ultimately developed. American Paleoarctic populations may have formed an impenetrable cultural, ecological, and technological wedge between Asia and North America that effectively blocked the spread into Asia of the waning Northern Paleoindian cultural tradition pursuing the remnant population of mammoth and other Pleistocene fauna that still persisted in the high northern latitudes.

Though this model accommodates colonization of the west coast of the Americas quite rapidly beginning about 14,000 B.P., it does not explain the earlier traces of human occupation that have been reported from the 32,000-year-old level at Monte Verde, the possible 33,000 B.P. at Pedra Furada, the circa 17,000 B.P. occupation at Meadowcroft Rock Shelter, and possibly other sites throughout the Americas that have been regarded as equivocal. If these early occupations withstand rigorous testing of the scientific criteria required to establish Pleistocene antiquity and validity as archeological sites, it will be necessary to accept the fact that humans had colonized South America by circa 35,000 B.P. and North America by circa 17,000 B.P. Though these sites may suggest that humans reached the Americas quite early, additional data will have to be amassed from other sites to fully evaluate the possibility.

CHAPTER 11

SPECULATIONS

 By midwinter I had completed many of my responsibilities, and it was time to bring to resolution and publication the controversial residue analysis of the fluted projectile points. Our entire family prepared to travel to Australia, where Tom Loy and I would wrap up our research. I had other motives for going to Australia. In addition to working with Loy, I wanted to learn if the peopling of Australia and islands of the South Pacific might provide insights helpful in understanding the earliest evidence for the peopling of the Americas. Although these vast continental land masses were at opposite ends of the globe, both had experienced similar phenomena; perhaps what was known from one might be applicable to understanding events on the other.

The day we were to leave Fairbanks for Australia, Dick Jordan died suddenly from a heart attack. His tragic and premature death shocked the community of arctic archeologists. When Jordan had been an undergraduate student at Dartmouth College, he had studied under Robert McKennan, who had excavated the Healy Lake Village site along with John Cook. From the summer I worked there I remember McKennan saying that a teacher lives on through his students and a researcher through his publications. I took comfort in the fact that Dick Jordan's academic legacy would survive through both his published research and the ongoing work of his students. The painful loss of a close friend and colleague made me realize how fortunate I had been to know so many of the colorful and dedicated scientists who have contributed to arctic archeology, and this instilled in me a sense of purpose to complete and publish the results of my ongoing research.

* * * * * * *

Upon our arrival at the Australia National University, Tom Loy and I resumed the work that we had begun with such enthusiasm

Chapter 11

four years earlier. I had shipped the residue samples ahead along with our original notes and documentation. We carefully began double-checking our work. From our original control sample of mammoth tissue we once again forced the growth of mammoth

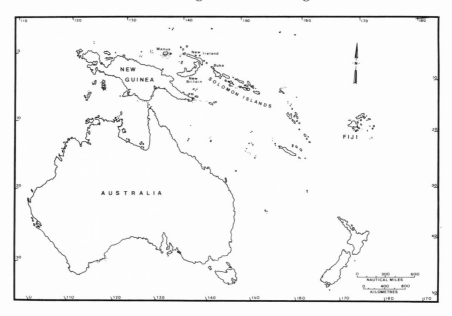

11.1 The western South Pacific, depicting islands on which Pleistocene age archeological sites have been discovered.

hemoglobin crystals. Although we lacked the equipment to do additional isoelectric focusing, we were able to replicate our earlier work from the original samples, which I had kept refrigerated over the past three years. Loy was more confident of his results. We worked on expanding our paper to more fully describe the methods and procedures. Because Loy was senior author, I left the manuscript with him to submit for publication.

While we were in Australia I had the opportunity to talk with other archeologists working in Austronesia, a term that applies to the combined regions of Australia and Polynesia. They guided me to some of the current regional archeological literature relevant to my areas of interest. Archeologists at Australia National University had

Speculations

been working on the southern rim of the Pacific Ocean, and I was curious about Pacific migrations and Pleistocene geology. As I talked with Rhys Jones and other leaders in Australian archeology, I was struck by the tremendous advances that had been made in the past 20 years. Just as the Bering Land Bridge was exposed by lower sea level during the last glaciation, so were the continental shelves of Australia. When sea level was lower, the islands of Tasmania and New Guinea were joined to Australia to form the Pleistocene continent called Sahul. A striking difference between Sahul and North America is the fact that Sahul was never connected to mainland Asia by a land bridge as North America had been. Australia could only have been colonized by humans who had the technology and capacity to cross open stretches of ocean.

In the mid 1960s (Mulvaney 1964), the first radiocarbon dates began to document the human occupation of Australia during the Pleistocene. Since that time a series of discoveries demonstrated human occupation throughout all areas of Sahul, and it became clear that during the Pleistocene humans had adapted to a vast array of environments from New Guinea in the north to Tasmania in the south. Rhys Jones (1989) suggests that the earliest dates for human occupation of the Australian continent exceed the effective limit of radiocarbon dating, which is approximately 40,000 years, and that the continent may have been occupied by humans much earlier.

As a Northern archeologist who knew little about the prehistory of this region, I was fascinated to learn of a series of remarkable discoveries made in the past decade that changed the interpretation of Austronesian prehistory. Prior to these discoveries, scientists thought the peopling of the Pacific islands was a relatively recent event. Since 1980 several important Pleistocene age archeological sites have been discovered on what are truly oceanic islands in the Pacific. In 1981 a date of circa 12,000 B.P. was reported for Misisil Cave in New Britain (Specht et al. 1981), and later Allen and his associates (1988, 1989) reported several Pleistocene sites from New Ireland. The oldest New Ireland site is Matenkupkum Cave, radiocarbon-dated to between 31,000 and 33,000 B.P. Wickler and Spriggs (1988) reported a 28,000 B.P. occupation from a rock shelter on Buka Island in the Solomons. Through the ongoing work of Wal Ambrose,

Chapter 11

Matthew Spriggs, and Clayton Fredericksen, the extent of Pleistocene occupation was expanded to the island of Manus in the Admiralty group, which is some 60–100 kilometers out of sight of the nearest islands (Spriggs 1992, personal communication 1991).

During the Pleistocene many Pacific islands were larger, and some were joined as a result of lower sea level (Gibbons and Clunie 1986). These more remote Pacific islands would have been easier targets for Pleistocene navigators because the distance between them was shorter and they were larger and higher above sea level. However, Irwin et al. (1990:38) indicate that favorable winds, currents, and frequency of bad weather were more important in sailing between islands than was reduced distance caused by lower sea level during the Pleistocene.

There are no archeological sites east of the Solomons that have been dated older than circa 3,500 B.P. This has led researchers (Irwin 1989, Jones 1989, Wickler and Spriggs 1988) to suggest that humans may have been unable to expand eastward beyond the Solomons because the ocean crossings beyond this point become increasingly difficult, the islands smaller and spread further apart. Additionally, these more remote islands tend to be impoverished in flora and fauna, offering a poor environment for humans.

Irwin (1989) has proposed the concept of a "voyaging nursery" in an island corridor extending from Southeast Asia to the end of the Solomon Islands, in which people could sail with relative safety between islands. He theorized that within these regions people were able to refine their sailing skills, their watercraft, and their navigational ability until by 3,500–4,000 B.P. they were able to venture beyond the "nursery" and colonize the other islands of the Pacific. This expansion, which began about 4,000 years ago, is linked to the concept of Lapita culture, which, in addition to its sailing ability, was able to carry and cultivate the necessary domestic plants and animals to make these rather depauperate islands productive enough to support human populations.

The rapid pace of archeological research throughout Austronesia documents what appears to be explosive human expansion from Asia that began at least 40,000 years ago. Humans were able to colonize not only Sahul but the oceanic islands of western Polynesia.

Speculations

There is no doubt that humans had the ability to successfully undertake relatively lengthy crossings between islands by this time. However, current archeological evidence suggests that this expansion did not go eastward into the Pacific and that navigators remained contained within their Pleistocene nursery for about 30,000 years until they had developed the skill to safely navigate the broader reaches of the Pacific.

Thirty thousand years is an incredibly long time from a human perspective. Could it be possible that some of these early navigators broke free from their Pleistocene nursery and somehow made their way across the Pacific to South America? Perhaps many such small events could have occurred, scattered over a period of more than 30,000 years, resulting in the human colonization of South America. If so, one would expect the archeological remains from the oldest levels at Monte Verde and Pedra Furada to look more like those of Pleistocene Austronesia than more widely recognized American traditions such as the Paleoindian.

It is possible that Pleistocene human occupations east of the Solomons have not been discovered because coastal sites dating to this time period may be submerged due to rising sea level at the end of the Pleistocene. Moreover, if such occupations had existed they may have been ephemeral and left little evidence in the archeological record. Until the 1980s no Pleistocene age sites were known from the oceanic islands of the Pacific. Future research may extend the eastward extent of sites, documenting an earlier human dispersal.

The idea of pre-Columbian transoceanic contacts between the New and Old Worlds is not popular among New World prehistorians. This results from the fact that many writers have abused the idea in an attempt to explain virtually every similarity, ranging from similarities in styles of art to the building of pyramids, between the two hemispheres on the basis of diffusion across the oceans. In the early 1980s I had published a popular article on the peopling of the Americas in which I merely hinted that humans may have colonized the Americas via the Pacific. I was sharply and swiftly criticized by several of my colleagues. One senior associate suggested that I not pursue this further for fear of losing my credibility within the profession.

Chapter 11

Because Native Americans are genetically most similar to modern Asiatic peoples, it has always been understood by anthropologists that the immigrants who populated the Americas must have come from Asia. Meltzer (1989) has written an article that explores the issues relating to why we do not know when humans first came to the Americas. In this excellent review, he points out that there is no need to think of human migration as specific events. Humans may have populated the Americas by migratory "dribbles" over long periods of time. Some of the migrations may have been successful, and others may not have been. Some of these small groups of early migrants could have been genetically swamped by later groups, possibly exterminated by warfare or the introduction of disease, may just have been too small to be viable, or perhaps died out from an inability to adapt to new environments.

Could humans have reached the Americas only to die out later or become genetically swamped by other human populations? By drawing on my knowledge of arctic archeology, I know the answer is yes. Circa A.D. 985, Erik the Red, a Norse exile from Iceland, led an expedition that colonized Greenland. About 15 years after the colony was established, the Vikings adopted Christianity. Surviving historic documents indicate that at one time the colony boasted a bishop, some 12 churches, a convent, and a monastery (Kleivan 1984:549). Archeological research has documented the ruins of at least 330 farms and 17 churches (Krogh 1982). Thousands of artifacts, including European-style clothing made of Greenland wool, have been found as well as the skeletons of the Vikings themselves. The colony persisted for about 500 years. But the last Norse colonists disappeared in the late 1400s, roughly the time Christopher Columbus was arriving in the Caribbean.

The disappearance of the Greenland Vikings is a topic that has captivated Western scholars for hundreds of years. Although many theories have been advanced to explain their disappearance, none is universally accepted. The analysis of human skeletons from both Norse and Inuit burials, as well as serological investigations, have failed to prove interbreeding between these two populations (Kleivan 1984:554). While the Norse expansion into the New World is a fascinating story in its own right, it also provides clear documenta-

Speculations

tion of a major and long-lived transoceanic colonization of the Americas that ultimately failed. Because Europeans and Inuits have continued to interbreed since A.D. 1600–1700, when Europeans once again colonized Greenland, it is impossible to tell whether European genetic traits in Inuit populations were derived from the Norse or later European explorers, whalers, or traders. Consequently, the original Norse colonization of Greenland cannot be demonstrated ever to have happened based on genetic analysis of living people.

The Norse phenomenon demonstrates that various groups of humans could have attempted colonization of the American continents, or even the more remote Pacific islands, only to subsequently disappear. If the immigrants were few in number, their technology largely of perishable organic material, and the length of their survival short, evidence of their passing would be extremely difficult to detect in the archeological record. As a result, New World prehistorians should not necessarily expect to find a continuous archeological record extending from the Pleistocene to the beginning of the well-documented archeological sites of the Llano and Nenana complexes. Perhaps sites such as Meadowcroft Rock Shelter are not to be understood as part of a monolithic model of the peopling of the Americas but are merely the tangible remains of sporadic early colonization events that were not connected to subsequent developments in New World prehistory. Although this is possible, my archeological experience indicates that it takes several discoveries before a pattern in the archeological record is identified and defined. Generally the first discoveries of different archeological material appear unique and difficult to explain until subsequent work reveals the larger cultural historical context of which it is a part.

The synthesis of the early archeology of eastern Beringia in chapter 10 provides a framework from which to interpret the late Pleistocene archeological data from northern North America. However, it does not explain the earlier traces of human occupation, which have been reported throughout the Americas. Could these sites be silent testimony to early but unsuccessful colonizations that failed, as did that of the Vikings thousands of years later? Are they

Chapter 11

perhaps evidence of successful crossings of the Pacific during the Pleistocene, which resulted first in the colonization of South America and subsequently North America? New World prehistorians should keep their minds open to these possibilities.

The evidence from Austronesia demonstrates that humans in the southern hemisphere were capable of making open water crossings as early as 35,000–40,000 years ago and that some of these were equivalent to those required to colonize the Americas along the margins of the North Pacific. Although it might be argued that the more mild tropical climates to the south rendered such crossings less hazardous, an appropriate level of adaptation to environmental circumstances in the North would make similar crossings possible along the North Pacific rim.

In a sense Austronesia is the mirror image of Beringia. The discoveries and insights from one hemisphere can contribute to understanding problems in the other. Remarkable progress has been made in both regions over the past two decades, enabling us to adopt a more global view of human migrations during the Pleistocene. This requires interdisciplinary research essential to interpret and provide the context for prehistoric mankind. New laboratories are needed to refine residue analysis and apply other as-yet-untapped biochemical methods to archeological problems. Advances will also require courage on the part of researchers who discover information that does not fit accepted scientific paradigms. These researchers must risk criticism and rejection from other scientists as they challenge accepted models and present alternative interpretations.

Essential to this progress is the flow of information between scientists to build the collective body of knowledge that continually reshapes our understanding of ourselves. Our knowledge results from the work of literally thousands of people involved in excavating, analyzing, and reporting archeological sites throughout the world. Synthesis is important to provide a framework for understanding the accumulated information. This in turn stimulates new interpretations and new hypotheses to be formulated and tested. Our knowledge expands and the cycle continues. Each aspect of scientific progress increases our understanding of the dispersal of

Speculations

mankind across the planet, but will the problem ever be fully understood and explained? I think not, because the quest will always pose new questions, and the quest is what is truly important.

BIBLIOGRAPHY

Ackerman, R. E.
   1968   *The Archeology of the Glacier Bay Region, Southeastern Alaska.* Report
           of Investigations No. 44. Washington State University,
           Laboratory of Anthropology, Pullman.

Ackerman, R.E., T.D. Hamilton, and R. Stuckenrath
   1979   Early Complexes on the Northern Northwest Coast. *Canadian
           Journal of Archaeology 3:195–208*

Ackerman, R. E., K. C. Reid, J. D. Gallison
and M. E. Roe.
   1985   *Archaeology of Heceta Island: A Survey of 18 Timber Harvest Units in
           the Tongass National Forest, Southeastern Alaska.* Center for
           Northwest Anthropology, Washington State University,
           Pullman.

Acosta, J., de
   1604   *The Naturall and Morall Historie of the East and West Indies.* Trans-
           lated by Edward Grimston. Reprinted by Bart Franklin, New
           York, by permission of the Haakluyt Society.

Adovasio, J. M., D. Gunn, J. Donahue, and R.
Stuckenrath
   1977   Meadowcroft Rockshelter: Retrospect 1976. *Pennsylvania Archae-
           ologist* 47(2–3):1–93.
   1978   Meadowcroft Rockshelter, 1977: An Overview. *American Antiquity*
           43:632–651.

Adovasio, J. M., J. D. Gunn, J. Donahue, R. Stuckenrath, J.
E. Guilday, and K. Lord
   1978   Meadowcroft Rockshelter. In *Early Man in the Americas from a
           Circum-Pacific Perspective,* edited by A. L. Bryan, 1:140–180.
           Occasional Papers of the Department of Anthropology,
           University of Alberta, Edmonton.

Adovasio, J., J. Gunn, J. Donahue, R. Stuckenrath, J.
E. Guilday, and K. Volman
   1980   Yes Virginia, It Really Is that Old: A Reply to Haynes and Mead.
           American Antiquity 45(3):588–595.

Aigner, J. S.
   1976   Dating the Early Holocene Maritime Village of
           Anangula. *Anthropological Papers of the University of Alaska* 18(1):51–
           62. Fairbanks.

Allen, J., C. Gosden, R. Jones, and J. P. White
   1988   Pleistocene Dates for Human Occupation of New Ireland,
           Northern Melanesia. *Nature* 331:707–709.

Bibliography

Allen, J., C. Gosden, and J. P. White
    1989   Pleistocene New Ireland. *Antiquity* 63(240):548–560.

Anderson, D. D.
    1968   A Stone Age Campsite at the Gateway to America. *Scientific American* 218(6):24–33.
    1970   Akmak: An Early Archeological Assemblage from Onion Portage, Northwest, Alaska. *Acta Arctica,* Fasc. XVI. København."
    1988   *Onion Portage: The Archaeology of a Stratified Site from the Kobuk River, Northwest Alaska.* Anthropological Papers of the University of Alaska 22(1–2). University of Alaska Press, Fairbanks.

Anderson, P. M.
    1985   Late-Quaternary Vegetational Changes in the Kotzebue Sound Area, Northwestern Alaska. *Quaternary Research* 24:307–321.

Behrensmeyer, A. K., and A. P. Hill
    1980   *Fossils in the Making. Vertebrate Taphonomy and Paleoecology.* University of Chicago Press, Chicago.

Blaise, B., J. J. Clague, and R. W. Mathewes
    1990   Time of Maximum Late Wisconsin Glaciation, West Coast of Canada. *Quaternary Research* 34:282–295.

Bobrowsky, P. T., N. R. Catto, J. W. Brink, B. E. Spurling, T. H. Gibson, and N.W. Rutter
    1990   *Archaeological Geology of Sites in Western and Northwestern Canada.* Centennial Special Volume 4, chapter 5, pp. 87–122. Geological Society of America, Boulder.

Bonnichsen, R.
    1978   Critical Arguments for Pleistocene Artifacts from the Old Crow Basin, Yukon: A Preliminary Statement. In *Early Man in America from a Circum-Pacific Perspective,* edited by A. L. Bryan, 1:102–118. Occasional Papers of the Department of Anthropology, University of Alberta, Edmonton.
    1979   *Pleistocene Bone Technology in the Beringian Refugium.* Archaeological Survey of Canada Paper 89. National Museum on Man, Mercury Series, Ottawa.

Bowers, P. M.
    1978a   Research Summary: 1977 Investigations of the Carlo Creek Archeological Site, Central Alaska. Ms. on file, University of Alaska Museum, Fairbanks.
    1978b   Abstract: Geology and Archaeology of the Carlo Site, a Stratified Early Holocene Campsite in the Central Alaska Range. Paper presented at the 31st Annual Northwest Anthropological Association Conference, Eugene. *Northwest Anthropological Re-*

Bibliography

search Notes 12(2):212.

1978c   Research Summary: 1977 Investigations of the Carlo Creek Archaeological Site, Central Alaska. Report submitted to the University of Alaska Museum, Fairbanks. Laboratory of Anthropology, Arctic Research Section, Washington State University, Pullman.

1980a   *The Carlo Creek Site: Geology and Archaeology of an Early Holocene Site in the Central Alaska Range.* Occasional Paper No. 27. Anthropology and Historic Preservation, Cooperative Park Studies Unit, Fairbanks.

1980b   *Management of Cultural Resources in the Proposed Western Arctic Management Area.* Draft report prepared for the Western Arctic Management Area Task Force Land Use Plan. U.S. Bureau of Land Management, Anchorage.

Bryan, A. (editor)

1978   *Early Man in the Americas from a Circum-Pacific Perspective.* Occasional Papers No. 1. Department of Anthropology, University of Alberta, Edmonton.

1986   *New Evidence for the Pleistocene Peopling of the Americas.* Center for the Study of Early Man, Orono.

Cinq-Mars, J.

1979   Bluefish Cave I: A Late Pleistocene Eastern Beringian Cave Deposit in the Northern Yukon. *Canadian Journal of Archaeology* 3:1–32.

Clague, J.J., et al.

1989   Quaternary Geology of the Canadian Cordillera. In *Quaternary Geology of Canada and Greenland,* R. J. Fulton, ed. Geological Society of Canada, Geology of Canada, no. 1, Ch. 1. Ottawa.

Clark, D. W.

1984   Northern Fluted Points: Paleo-Eskimo, Paleo-Arctic, or Paleo-Indian. *Canadian Journal of Anthropology* 4(1):65–81.

1984   Some Practical Applications of Obsidian Hydration Dating in the Subarctic. *Arctic* 37(2):91–109.

Colinvaux, P. A.

1964   The Environment of the Bering Land Bridge. *Ecological Monographs* 34(3):297–329.

Colinvaux, P. A., and F. H. West

1984   The Beringian Ecosystem. *Quarterly Review of Archaeology* 5(3)10–16.

Cook, J. P.

1969   *The Early Prehistory of Healy Lake, Alaska.* Ph.D. dissertation. Department of Anthropology, University of Wisconsin, Madison.

Cook, J. P., and R. A. McKennan

1970   The Village Site at Healy Lake, Alaska: An Interim Report. Paper read at the 35th Annual Meeting of the Society for American Archeologists, Mexico City, Mexico.

Cwynar, L. C.

Bibliography

1982   A Late-Quaternary Vegetation History from Hanging Lake, North
ern Yukon. *Ecological Monographs* 52:1–24.

Cwynar, L. C., and J. C. Ritchie
    1980   Arctic Steppe-Tundra: a Yukon Perspective. *Science*
    208:375–377.

Davis, S. D.
    1989   Cultural Component I. In *The Hidden Falls Site,* edited by Stanley
    D. Davis, pp. 159–198. Monograph Series No. 5. Alaska Anthro-
    pological Association, Aurora.

Dawson, G. M.
    1894   Geological Notes on Some of the Coasts and Islands of Bering Sea
    and Vicinity. *Geological Society of America Bulletin* 5:117–146.

Deetz, J.
    1967   *Invitation to Archaeology.* American Museum Science Books. The
    Natural History Press, Garden City, New York.

Dikov, N. N.
    1977   *Arkheologicheshie pamyatniki Kamchctki, Chukotki i Verkhnej Kolymy*
    (Archeological Monuments of Kamchatka, Chukotka, and the
    Upper Kolyma). Nauka, Moscow.
    1979   *Drevnie kul'tury Severo-Vostochnoj Azii* (Ancient Cultures of North-
    east Asia). Nauka, Moscow.

Dikov, N. N., and E. E. Titov
    1984   Problems of the Stratification and Periodization of the Ushki Sites.
    Arctic Anthropology 21(2):69–80.

Dillehay, T. D.
    1984   A Late Ice-Age Settlement in Southern Chile. *Scientific American*
    251(4):100–109.
    1988   How New is the New World? *Antiquity* 62:94–97.

Dillehay, T. D., and M. Collins
    1988   Early Cultural Evidence from Monte Verde in Chile. *Nature*
    332:150–152.

Dixon, E. J.
    1975   The Gallagher Flint Station, An Early Man Site on the North Slope,
    Arctic Alaska, and its Role in Relation to the Bering Land Bridge.
    Arctic Anthropology 12(1):68–75.
    1976   The Pleistocene Prehistory of Arctic North America In *Colloque
    XVII Habitats Humains. Anterieurs a l'Holocene en Amerique,* edited
    by J. B. Griffin, pp. 168–198. Proceedings of the IX International
    Congress of Anthropological Sciences, Nice, France.
    1983   Pleistocene Proboscidean Fossils from the Alaskan Continental
    Shelf. *Quaternary Research* 20(1):113–119.
    1984   Context and Environment in Taphonomic Analysis: Examples
    from Alaska's Porcupine River Caves. *Quaternary Research* 22:201–
    215.
    1985   Cultural Chronology of Central Interior Alaska. *Arctic Anthro-*

Bibliography

pology 22(1):47–66.

1986   The Northern Paleoindian/Northern Archaic Transition in Alaska. Paper presented at the 13th Annual Meeting of the Alaska Anthropological Association, Fairbanks, Alaska.

Dixon, E. J., D. C. Plaskett, and R. M. Thorson

1985   *Cave Deposits, Porcupine River Alaska.* National Geographic Society Research Reports, 1979 Projects, Washington, D.C.

Dixon, E. J., and G. S. Smith

1986   Broken Canines from Alaskan Cave Deposits: Re-evaluating Evidence for Domesticated Dog and Early Humans in Alaska. *American Antiquity* 51:341–351.

1990   *A Regional Application of Tephrochronology in Alaska,* Centennial Special Volume 4, chapter 21, pp. 383–398. Geological Society of America, Boulder.

Dixon, E. J., and R. M. Thorson

1984   Taphonomic Analysis and Interpretation in North American Pleistocene Archaeology. *Quaternary Research* 22:155–159.

Dumond, D. E.

1977   *The Eskimos and Aleuts.* Thames and Hudson, London.

1980   The Archeology of Alaska and the Peopling of America. *Science* 209:984–991.

1982   Trends and Traditions in Alaskan Prehistory: The Place of Norton Culture. *Arctic Anthropology* 19(2):39–51.

Dumond, D. E., W. Henn, and R. Stuckenrath

1976   Archaeology and Prehistory on the Alaska Peninsula. *Anthropological Papers of the University of Alaska* 18(1):17–29.

Elias, S. A., S. K. Short, and R. L. Phillips

1992   Paleoecology of Late Glacial Peats from the Bering Land Bridge, Chukchi Sea Shelf Region, Northwestern Alaska. *Quaternary Research.*

Fagan, B. M.

1987   *The Great Journey: the Peopling of Ancient America.* Thames & Hudson, London and New York.

Fladmark, K. R.

1979   Routes: Alternative Migration Corridors for Early Man in North America. *American Antiquity* 44:55–69.

1980-81 *Paleo-Indian Artifacts from the Peace River District.* Special Issue of BC Studies No. 48, pp. 124–135. University of British Columbia Press, Vancouver.

1983   Times and Places: Environmental Correlates of Mid-to-Late Wisconsin Human Population Expansion in North America. In *Early Man in the New World,* edited by Richard Shutler, pp. 13–42. Sage Publication, Beverly Hills.

1986   Getting One's Berings. *Natural History* 95(11):8-19.

Gibbons, J. R. H., and G. A. U. Clunie

Bibliography

1986   Sea Level Changes and Pacific Prehistory, New Insight into Early Human Settlement of Oceania. *The Journal of Pacific History* 21(2):58–82, Oxford Press, Melbourne.

Gifford, J. A., and G. Rapp, Jr.
1985   The Early Development of Archaeological Geology in North America. In *Geologists and Ideas: A History of North American Geology,* edited by Ellen T. Drake and William M. Jordan, pp. 409–422. Centennial Special Volume 1. Geological Society of America, Boulder, Colorado.

Goebel, F. E., and W. R. Powers
1990   Early Paleoindians in Beringia and the Origins of Clovis. In *Chronostratigraphy of the Paleolithic of North, Central and East Asia and America,* p. 173. Academy of Sciences of the USSR Institute of History, Philology and Philosophy, Siberian Branch of the Academy of Sciencies. Novosibirsk, USSR.

Goebel, F. E., W. R. Powers, and N. Bigelow
1991   The Nenana Complex of Alaska and Clovis Origins. In *Clovis Origins and Adaptations,* edited by R. Bonnichsen and K. Turnmire, pp. 49–79. Center for the Study of the First Americans, Oregon State University, Corvalis.

Goebel, F. E., and W. R. Powers
1989   A Possible Paleo Indian Dwelling in the Nenana, Alaska: Spatial Analysis at the Walker Road Site. Paper presented at the 16th Annual Meeting of the Alaska Anthropological Association, Fairbanks.

Guidon, N., and G. Delibrias
1986   Carbon-14 Dates Point to Man in the Americas 32,000 Years Ago. *Nature* 321:769–771.

Guthrie, M. L.
1988   *Blue Babe: The Story of a Steppe Bison Mummy from Ice Age Alaska.* White Mammoth, Fairbanks.

Guthrie, R. D.
1968   Paleoecology of the Large Mammal Community in Interior Alaska during the Late Pleistocene. *The American Midland Naturalist* 79(2):346–363.
1982   Mammals of the Mammoth Steppe as Paleoenvironmental Indicators. In *Paleoecology of Beringia,* edited by D. M. Hopkins, J. V. Matthews, Jr., C. E. Schweger, and S. B. Young, pp. 307–326. Academic Press, New York.
1985   Pleistocene Paleontology. Woolly Arguments Against the Mammoth Steppe—A New Look at the Palynological Data. *Quarterly Review of Archeology* 6(3):9–16.
1990   *Frozen Fauna of the Mammoth Steppe.* University of Chicago Press, Chicago.

Hamilton, T. D.

Bibliography

1970 Geologic Relations of the Akmak Assemblage, Onion Portage Area. Appendix, pp.71–78. *Acta Arctica,* Fasc. XVI, København.

Harington, C. R.
 1977 *Pleistocene mammals of the Yukon Territory.* Ph.D. dissertation, University of Alberta, Edmonton.
 1978 *Quaternary Vertebrate Faunas of Canada and Alaska and Their Suggested Chronological Sequence.* Canadian National Museum of Natural Sciences, Syllogeus 15, Ottawa.
 1980a Pleistocene Mammals from Lost Chicken Creek, Alaska. *Canadian Journal of Earth Sciences* 17:168–198.
 1980b Radiocarbon Dates on Some Quaternary Mammals and Artifacts from Northern North America. *Arctic* 33(81):5–32.

Harington, C. R., and D. M. Shackleton
 1978 A Tooth of *Mammuthus Primigenius* from Chestermere Lake near Calgary, Alberta, and the Distribution of Mammoths in Southwestern Canada. *Canadian Journal of Earth Sciences* 15:1272–1283.

Hassan, A. A., and D. J. Ortner
 1977 Inclusions in Bone Material as a Source of Error in Radiocarbon Dating. *Archaeometry* 19:131–135.

Hassan, A. A., and P. E. Hare
 1978 Amino Acid Analysis in Radiocarbon Dating of Bone Collagen. Advances in Chemistry Series 171. *Archeological Chemistry* 11:109–116.

Haynes, C. V., Jr.
 1964 Fluted Projectile Points: Their Age and Dispersion. *Science* 145:14098–113.
 1987 Clovis Origin Update. *The Kiva* 52(2):83–92.

Haynes, C. V., Jr., D. C. Grey, and A. Long
 1971 Arizona Radiocarbon Dates VIII. *Radiocarbon* 13:1–18.

Henn, W.
 1978 *Archaeology on the Alaska Peninsula: The Ugashik Drainage.* 1973–1975. Anthropological Papers No. 14. University of Oregon, Eugene.

Hester, J. J.
 1960 The Late Pleistocene Extinctions. *American Antiquity* 26:58–87.

Hester, J. J., and J. Grady
 1982 *Introduction to Archaeology.* 2 ed. Chapter 10, p. 169. Holt, Rinehart and Winston, New York.

Holmes, C. E.
 1988 An Early Post Paleo-Arctic Site in the Alaska Range. Paper presented at the 15th Annual Meeting of the Alaska Anthropological Association, Fairbanks.
 1990 The Broken Mammoth Site: Its Relevance in Alaska/Yukon Prehistory. Paper presented at the Canadian Archaeological Association

Bibliography

Annual Meeting, Whitehorse, Yukon Territory.

Holmes, C.E., and G. Bacon
1982   Holocene Bison in Central Alaska: A Possible Explanation for Technological Conservatism. Paper presented at the 9th Annual Meeting of the Alaska Anthropological Association, Fairbanks.

Holmes, C. E., R. J. Dale, and J. D. McMahn
1989   *Archaeological Mitigation of the Thorne River Site* (CRG–177). Office of History and Archaeology Report No. 15. Division of Parks and Outdoor Recreation, Alaska Department of Natural Resources.

Hopkins, D. M.
1963   *Geology of Imuruk Lake Area, Seward Peninsula, Alaska.* USGS Bulletin No. 1141, C1-C101.

1967   *The Bering Land Bridge.* Stanford University Press, Stanford.

1973   Sea Level History in Beringia during the Past 250,000 Years. *Quaternary Research* 3(4):520–540.

1979   Landscape and Climate of Beringia during Late Pleistocene and Holocene Times. In *The First Americans: Origins, Affinities, and Adaptations,* edited by William S. Laughlin and Albert B. Harper, pp.15–41. Gustav Fischer, New York.

1982   Aspects of the Paleogeography of Beringia during the Late Pleistocene. In *Paleoecology of Beringia,* edited by D. M. Hopkins, J. V. Matthews, Jr., C. E. Schweger, and S. B. Young, pp. 3–28. Academic Press, New York.

Irving, W. N., and C. R. Harington
1973   Upper Pleistocene Radiocarbon-Dated Artifacts from the Northern Yukon. January 26. *Science* 179:335–340.

Irwin, G.
1989   Against, Across and Down the Wind: A Case for the Systematic Exploration of the Remote Pacific Islands. *The Journal of the Polynesian Society* 98(2):167–206.

Irwin, G., S. Bickler, and P. Quirke
1990   Voyaging by Canoe and Computer: Experiments in the Settlement of the Pacific Ocean. *Antiquity* 64(242):34–50.

Johnston, W. A.
1933   *Quaternary Geology of North America in Relation to the Migration of Man: The American Aborigines, Their Origins and Antiquity.* Edited by Diamond Jenness, pp. 9–46. University of Toronto Press, Toronto.

Jones, R.
1989   East of Wallace's Line: Issues and Problems in the Colonisation of the Australian Continent. In *The Human Revolution,* edited by P. Mellars and C. Stringer, pp. 743–782. University of Edinburgh Press and Princeton University Press, Edinburgh and Princeton.

Jopling, A. V., W. N. Irving, and B. F. Beebe
1981   Stratigraphic, Sedimentological and Faunal Evidence for the Occurrence of Pre-Sangamonian Artifacts in Northern Yukon. *Arctic*

Bibliography

34(1):3–33.

Jordan, R. H.
1992   A Maritime Paleoarctic Assemblage from Kodiak Island, Alaska. Vol. 24 Nos. 1 and 2. Anthropological Papers of the University of Alaska, Fairbanks.

Kleivan, I.
1984   History of Norse Greenland. In *Arctic,* edited by D. Damas, pp. 549–555. Handbook of North American Indians, volume 5, W. Sturtevant, general editor. Smithsonian Institution, Washington, D.C.

Krogh, K. J.
1982   *Gronland: Erik den Rodes Gronland* (Eric the Red's Greenland). 2d rev. ed. Nationalmuseet, Copenhagen.

Larsen, H.
1968a   Trail Creek, Final Report on the Excavation of Two Caves at Seward Peninsula, Alaska. *Acta Arctica* 15:7–79. København.
1968b   The Eskimo Culture and Its Relationship to Northern Eurasia. In *Proceedings of the VIIIth International Congress of Anthropological and Ethnological Sciences,* edited by Banri Endo, Hiroshi Hoshi, and Shozo Masuda 3:337–340. Tokyo and Kyoto.

Laughlin, S. B., W. S. Laughlin, and M. W. McDowell
1975   Anangula Blade Site Excavations, 1972 and 1973. *Anthropological Papers of the University of Alaska,* 17(2):39–48.

Laughlin, W. S.
1967   Human Migration and Permanent Occupation in the Bering Area. In *The Bering Land Bridge,* edited by D. M. Hopkins, pp. 409–450. Stanford University Press, Stanford.
1975   Aleuts: Ecosystem, Holocene History, and Siberian Origin. *Science* 189 (4202):507–515.

Lively, R.
1988   *Chugwater (FAI–035): A Study of the Effectiveness of a Small Scale Probabilistic Sampling Design at an Interior Alaskan Site.* Chena River Lakes Flood Control Project. US Army Corps of Engineers, Alaska District.

Loy, T. H.
1983   Prehistoric Blood Residues: Detection on Tool Surfaces and Identification of Species of Origin. *Science* 220:1269–1271.

Loy, T. H., and A. R. Wood
1989   Blood residue analysis at Cayonu Tepesi, Turkey. *Journal of Field Archaeology* 16(4):451–460.

MacDonald, G. M.
1987a   Postglacial Development of the Subalpine-Boreal Transition Forest of Western Canada. *Journal of Ecology* 75:303–320.
1987b   Postglacial Vegetation History of the Mackenzie River Basin. *Quaternary Research* 28(2):245–262.

Bibliography

McManus, D. A., J. S. Creager, R. J. Echols, and M. L. Holmes
  1983 The Holocene Transgression of the Arctic Flank of Beringia:
        Chukchi Valley to Chukchi Estuary to Chukchi Sea. In *Quaternary
        Coastlines and Marine Archeology,* edited by P. M. Masters and M.
        C. Flemming, pp. 365–388. Academic Press, New York.

Marshall, E.
  1990 Clovis Counterrevolution. *Science,* 249:738–741.

Martin, P. J.
  1982 Digestive and Grazing Strategies of Animals in the Arctic Steppe.
        In *Paleoecology of Beringia,* edited by David M. Hopkins, John V.
        Matthews, Jr., Charles E. Schweger, and Steven B. Young, pp. 259–
        266. Academic Press, New York.

Martin, P. S.
  1967 Prehistoric Overkill. In *Pleistocene Extinctions: The Search for a
        Cause,* edited by P. S. Martin and H. E. Wright, pp. 75–120. Yale
        University Press, New Haven, Conn.
  1973 The Discovery of America. *Science,* 179:969–974.
  1982 Pattern and Meaning of Holarctic Mammoth Extinction. In
        Paleoecology of Beringia, edited by D. M. Hopkins, J. V. Matthews,
        Jr., C. E. Schweger, and S. B. Young, pp. 399–408. Academic Press,
        New York.
  1984 Prehistoric Extinctions: The Global Model. In *Quaternary
        Extinctions: A Prehistoric Revolution,* edited by P. S. Martin and R.
        G. Klein, pp. 354–403. University of Arizona Press, Tucson.

Mehringer, P. J., Jr., and F. F. Foit, Jr.
  1990 Volcanic Ash Dating of the Clovis Cache at East Wenatchee,
        Washington. *National Geographic Research* 6(4):495–503.

Meltzer, D. J.
  1989 Why Don't We Know When the First People Came to North
        America? *American Antiquity* 54:471–490.

Michael, H. N.
  1984 Absolute Chronologies of Late Pleistocene and Early Holocene
        Cultures of Northeastern Asia. *Arctic Anthropology* 21(2):1–68.

Mochanov, Y. A.
  1977 *Drevnejshie etapy zaseleniya chelovekom Severo-Vostochnoj Azii* (An-
        cient-Most Stages of the Settlement by Man of Northeast Asia).
        Nauka, Novosibirsk.

Morlan, R. E.
  1977 Fluted Point Makers and the Extinction of the Arctic-Steppe
        Biome in Eastern Beringia. *Canadian Journal of Archaeology*
        1:95–108.
  1980 Taphonomy and Archaeology in the Upper Pleistocene of the
        Northern Yukon Territory: A Glimpse of the Peopling of the New
        World. *National Museum of Man Mercury Series,* Archaeological
        Survey of Canada Paper No. 94. Ottawa.

144

Bibliography

Morlan, R. E., and J. Cinq-Mars
   1982   Ancient Beringians: Human Occupation in the Late Pleistocene of
           Alaska and the Yukon Territory. In *Paleoecology of Beringia,* edited
           by D. M. Hopkins et al., pp. 353–381. Academic Press, New York.
Mosimann, J. E., and P. S. Martin
   1975   Simulating Overkill by Paleoindians. *American Scientist* 63:304–
           313.
Müller-Beck, H. J.
   1966   Paleohunters in America: Origins and Diffusion. *Science*
           152(3726):1191–1210.
   1967   Migrations of Hunters on the Land Bridge in the Upper Pleisto-
           cene. In *The Bering Land Bridge,* edited by D. M. Hopkins, pp. 373–
           408. Stanford University Press, Stanford, California.
Mulvaney, D. J.
   1964   The Pleistocene Colonization of Australia. *Antiquity* 38:263–267.
Nelson, D. E., R. E. Morlan, J. S. Vogel, J. R. Southon, and C. R. Harington
   1986   New Dates on Northern Yukon Artifacts: Holocene Not Upper
           Pleistocene. *Science* 232:749–51.
Nelson, N. C.
   1933   The Antiquity of Man in America in the Light of Archaeology. In
           The American Aborigines, Their Origin and Antiquity, edited by
           Diamond Jenness, pp. 373–396. University of Toronto Press,
           Toronto.
   1935   Early Migration of Man to America. *Natural History* 35(4):356.
   1937   Notes on Cultural Relations between Asia and America. *American
           Antiquity* 2(4):267–272.
Okada, H., A. Okada, Y. Kotani, K. Yajima, W. M. Olson, Y. Nishimoto,
and S. Okino
   1989   *Heceta Island, Southeastern Alaska Anthropological Survey in 1987.*
           Department of Behavioral Science, Faculty of Letters, Hokkaido
           University, Sapporo, Japan.
Owen-Smith, N.
   1987   Pleistocene Extinctions: The Pivotal Role of Megaherbivores.
           Paleobiology 13(3):351–362.
Pewe, T. L.
   1975a   Quaternary Geology of Alaska. *U. S. Geological Survey Professional
           Paper* 835:1–145.
   1975b   Quaternary Stratigraphic Nomenclature in Unglaciated Central
           Alaska. *U.S. Geological Survey Professional Paper* 862:1–32.
Pewe, T. L., D. M. Hopkins, and J. L. Giddings
   1965   The Quaternary Geology and Archeology of Alaska. In *The
           Quaternary of the United States: A Review Volume for the VII Congress
           of the International Association for Quaternary Research,* edited by H.
           E. Wright, Jr. and D. G. Frey, pp. 355–374. Princeton University
           Press, Princeton.

Bibliography

Phippen, P. G.
1988   *Archaeology at Owl Ridge: A Pleistocene-Holocene Boundary Age Site in Central Alaska.* M.A. thesis, University of Alaska, Fairbanks.
Powers, W. R.
1973   Paleolithic Man in Northeast Asia. *Arctic Anthropology* 10(2):1–106.
1990   The People of Eastern Beringia. *Prehistoric Mongoloid Dispersals,* No. 7.
Powers, W. R., and J. F. Hoffecker
1989   Late Pleistocene Settlement in the Nenana Valley, Central Alaska. *American Antiquity* 54(2):263–287.
Powers, W. R., and H. E. Maxwell
1986   *Lithic Remains from Panguingue Creek: An Early Holocene Site in the Northern Foothills of the Alaska Range.* Alaska Historical Commission, Anchorage.
Prest, V. K.
1984   The Late Wisconsinan Glacier Complex. In *Quaternary Stratigraphy of Canada — A Canadian Contribution to IGCP Project 24,* edited by R. J. Fulton, pp. 21–36. Geological Survey of Canada Paper 84–10. Ottawa.
Rainey, F.
1939   Archaeology in Central Alaska. *Anthropological Papers of the American Museum of Natural History* 36(4):351–405.
Redman, R. E.
1982   Production and Diversity in Contemporary Grasslands. In *Paleoecology of Beringia,* edited by D. M. Hopkins, J. V. Matthews, Jr., C. E. Schweger, and S. B. Young, pp. 223–240. Academic Press, New York.
Reger, D. R.
1981   *A Model for Culture History in Upper Cook Inlet, Alaska.* Unpublished Ph.D. dissertation, Department of Anthropology, Washington State University, Pullman.
Repenning, C.A., D. M. Hopkins, and M. Rubin
1964   Tundra Rodents in a Late Pleistocene Fauna from the Tofty Placer District, Central Alaska. *Arctic* 17(3):177-197.
Ritchie, J. C.
1984   *Past and Present Vegetation of the Far Northwest of Canada.* University of Toronto Press, Toronto.
Ritchie, J. C., and L. C. Cwynar
1982   The Late Quaternary Vegetation of the North Yukon. In *Paleoecology of Beringia,* edited by D. M. Hopkins, J. V. Matthews, Jr., C. E. Schweger, and S. B. Young, pp. 113–126. Academic Press, New York.
Rutherford, A. A., J. Wittenberg, and K. J. McCallum
1973   University of Saskatchewan Radiocarbon Dates VI. *Radiocarbon*

Bibliography

15:193–211.

Rutter, N.W.
1984   Pleistocene History of the Western Canadian Ice-Free Corridor. In *Quaternary Stratigraphy of Canada—A Canadian Contribution to I GCP Project 24*, edited by R. J. Fulton, pp. 49–56. Geological Survey of Canada Paper 84–10, Ottawa.

Sattler, R. A.
1991   *Paleoecology of A Late Quaternary Cave Deposit in Northeast Alaska.* M.S. thesis, University of Alaska, Fairbanks.

Schaaf, Jeanne
1988   *The Bering Land Bridge National Perserve: An Archeological Survey* Vol 1. National Park Service—Alaska Region. Research/Resources Management Report AR–14

Schweger, C.
1982   Primary Production and Pleistocene Ungulates—The Productivity Paradox. In *Paleoecology of Beringia*, edited by D. M. Hopkins, J. V. Matthews, Jr., C. E. Schweger, and S. B. Young, pp. 95–112. Academic Press, New York.

Shutler, R., Jr.
1983   The Australian Parallel to the Peopling of the New World. In *Early Man in the New World,* edited by R. Shutler, Jr., pp. 43–46. Sage Publications, Beverly Hills.

Sinclair, A., and W. Slattery
1982   Identification of Meat According to Species by Isoelectric Focusing. *Australian Veterinary Journal* 58:77–80.

Specht, J., I. Lilley, and J. Normu
1981   Radiocarbon Dates from West New Britain. Papua, New Guinea. *Australian Archaeology* 12:13–15.

Spinden, H. J.
1933   Origin of Civilization in Central America and Mexico. In *The American Aborigines, Their Origin and Antiquity,* edited by Diamond Jenness, pp. 217–246. University of Toronto Press, Toronto.

Spriggs, M.
In Press The Lapita Culture and Austronesian Prehistory in Oceania. In *The Austronesians in History: Common Origins and Diverse Transformations,* edited by P. Bellwood, J. Fox, and D. Tryon.

Stanford, D.
1979   Afterward: Resolving the Question of New World Origins. In *Pre-Llano Cultures of the Americas: Paradoxes and Possibilities,* edited by R. L. Humphrey and D. Stanford, pp. 147–152. The Anthropological Society of Washington, Washington, D.C.
1983   Pre-Clovis Occupation South of the Ice Sheets. In *Early Man in the New World,* edited by Richard Shutler, Jr., pp. 65–72. Sage Publications, Beverly Hills.

Bibliography

Tauber, H.
  1973   Copenhagen Radiocarbon Dates X. *Radiocarbon* 15:107.
Thorson, R. M., and R. D. Guthrie
  1984   River Ice as a Taphonomic Agent: An Alternative Hypothesis for Bone "Artifacts." *Quaternary Research* 22:172–188.
Thorson, R. M., and T. D. Hamilton
  1977   Geology of the Dry Creek Site: A Stratified Early Man Site in Interior Alaska. *Quaternary Research* 7:149–176.
Thorson, R. M., D. C. Plaskett, and E. J. Dixon
  1980   A Reported Early Man Site Adjacent to Southern Alaska's Continental Shelf: A Geologic Solution to an Archeologic Enigma. *Quaternary Research* 13:259–273.
Ukraintseva, V. V.
  1985   Forage of the Large Herbivorous Mammals of the Epoch of the Mammoth. *Acta Zool. Fennica* 170:215–220.
Vinson, D.
  1988   Preliminary Report on Faunal Identifications from Trail Creek Caves. In *The Bering Land Bridge National Preserve: An Archeological Survey,* edited by J. Schaaf, volume 1, pp. 410–438. National Park Service, Anchorage.
Waters, M. R.
  1985   Early Man in the New World: An Evaluation of the Radiocarbon Dated Pre-Clovis Sites in the Americas. In *Environments and Extinctions: Man in the Late Glacial North America,* edited by Jim I. Mead and David J. Meltzer, pp. 125–143. Center for the Study of Early Man, University of Maine, Orono.
West, F. H.
  1973   Old World Affinities of Archaeological Complexes from Tangle Lakes, Central Alaska. Paper presented at the International Conference on the Bering Land Bridge and Its Role for the History of Holarctic Floras and Faunas in the Late Cenozoic, Khabarovsk, USSR.
  1975   Dating the Denali Complex. *Arctic Anthropology* 12(1):76–81.
  1981   *The Archaeology of Beringia.* Columbia University Press, New York.
Wickler, S., and M. Spriggs
  1988   Pleistocene Human Occupation of the Solomon Islands, Melanesia. *Antiquity* 62:703–706.

INDEX

Index

Index

Index

Ice Ages. *See* Pleistocene
Ice free corridor, 20, 22–23, 118, 119; radiocarbon dates for, 22. *See also* Paleoindian
    tradition
Iceland, 130
Inuit culture, 66, 130
Irving, William, 41–42, 50
Isoelectric focusing (IEF), 70, 74–75, 106, 126. *See also* Blood residue analysis
Isoelectric point (Pi), 70, 75. *See also* Blood residue analysis

Johnston, W. A., 5–6, 20
Jones, Rhys, 126–27
Jordan, Richard, 62–64, 77–78, 98, 101, 105, 112, 120, 125
Juneau, Alaska, 63

Larsen, Helge, 54–56, 61–62, 65–66, 78, 118
Laughlin, William, 62
Lively, Ralph, 82
Llano complex, 16, 103, 112, 131; and American Paleoarctic tradition, 67; and Nenana
    complex, 94, 123; and Northern Paleoindian tradition, 23, 109
Loy, Thomas, 12–13, 24, 67, 69–70, 73–75, 77, 86, 105–6, 109–13, 125–26

McKennan, Robert, 125
Mammoth, 5, 11, 24, 48, 67, 75, 112, 123–24; associated with projectile points, 8, 11, 16, 75,
    106, 109; in the Birch interval, 33–34; in eastern Beringia, 28, 86; hemoglobin, 13, 71,
    73, 106, 108, 126; hunted by early Americans, 9, 23, 29, 66, 84, 94, 112, 116, 118. *See
    also* American Museum of Natural History, Beringia, Blood residue analysis, Clovis,
    Holocene, Nenana complex, Pleistocene

Mammuthus primigenius. See Mammoth
Maritime Paleoarctic tradition. *See* American Paleoarctic tradition
Martin, Paul S., 9–10, 122
Mastodon, 5; hunted by early Americans, 84; at Monte Verde, 96–97
Matthews, John, *The Paleoecology of Beringia,* 11
Meltzer, D. J., 122, 129
Microblades, 83, 121; absent in Nenana complex sites, 82, 83, 86–89, 116; in Siberia, 121
Minimum limiting date: for animal extinction, 29–30; for human occupation
    (Kodiac Island), 63
Morlan, Richard, 50, 77
Mosimann, J. E., 10, 122
Müller-Beck, Hans Jurgen, 93–94

National Geographic Society, 23
National Museum of Man, Ottawa, Ontario, 15, 67, 69, 77
National Oceanic and Atmospheric Administration, 11

Index

Index

Quest for the Origins of the First Americans was
designed by Harold Augustus
and composed on a Macintosh IIci computer using
PageMaker 4.2, with 11/14 Stone Serif from the Adobe Library.
Outputted on a Linotronic L300,
it was printed and bound by Thomson-Shore Inc.,
on 50lb Natural offset.